Scottish Band of Hope Union.

Instituted 1871.

School Lectures Department.

Lectures on Temperance,

as per Syllabus, Scotch Education Dept.

Prize

AWARDED TO

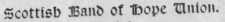

Robt. Watt.

FOR

Essay on

Temperance

WITH THE DIRECTORS' COMPLIMENTS
AND BEST WISHES.

PETER M'DONALD. SECY.

....Headmaster

R. Corbie...Lecturer

38 Bath Street,

Glasgow,.........................19

THE MAKING OF SCOTLAND

PUBLISHED BY

JAMES MACLEHOSE AND SONS, GLASGOW,

Publishers to the University.

———

MACMILLAN AND CO., LTD., LONDON.

New York, - -	*The Macmillan Co.*
Toronto, - - -	*The Macmillan Co. of Canada.*
London, - - -	*Simpkin, Hamilton and Co.*
Cambridge, - -	*Bowes and Bowes.*
Edinburgh, - -	*Douglas and Foulis.*
Sydney, - - -	*Angus and Robertson.*

———

MCMXI.

THE MAKING OF SCOTLAND

LECTURES ON THE WAR OF INDEPENDENCE
DELIVERED IN THE UNIVERSITY
OF GLASGOW

BY THE RIGHT HON.

SIR HERBERT MAXWELL, Bt.

F.R.S., LL.D. (Glasgow), D.C.L. (Durham)
PRES. SOC. ANT. SCOT.

GLASGOW
JAMES MACLEHOSE AND SONS
PUBLISHERS TO THE UNIVERSITY

1911

GLASGOW: PRINTED AT THE UNIVERSITY PRESS
BY ROBERT MACLEHOSE AND CO. LTD.

Contents

Illustrations

Introduction

IN the following pages I have endeavoured to range in a concise form the facts, so far as they can be ascertained, leading to the evolution of the realm of Scotland by the consolidation of the petty kingdoms which existed in the eighth century, the events which subsequently infringed and threatened permanently to destroy its independence, and the means by which that independence was regained and established. The narrative has been told and retold very often, varying in accordance with the prepossession, prejudice and historical insight of different writers ; yet it remains a fact that, while many Scotsmen desire to have a definite understanding of the cause for which their forefathers made such heavy sacrifice, few can give the time necessary for the examination and collation of conflicting authorities. I have attempted, therefore, to put the essence of the matter into these lectures, and, at the same time, to convey some impression of the kind of warfare whereby our independence was secured.

Every question has at least two sides; that which arose in the thirteenth century between England and Scotland has too often been treated as if it had only one. We are now far enough removed from the field of strife to take a just view of the English, as well as the Scottish, aspect of the controversy.

As I have dealt with the War of Independence in greater detail in a volume on *Robert the Bruce* contributed to the "Heroes of the Nation" series in 1897, I have to acknowledge the courtesy with which the publishers, Messrs. G. P. Putnam's Sons, have consented to waive any objection they might entertain to such repetition as has been found inevitable. I have not in most cases supplied references to the various authorities upon which the statements in the text are based, because the lectures are

INTRODUCTION

printed almost *literatim* as delivered, and such references would have unnecessarily confused an oral narrative. The chief authorities relied on have been Bain's *Calendar of Documents relating to Scotland*, Lord Hailes's *Annals of Scotland*, Rymer's *Fœdera Antiqua*, Barbour's *Brus*, *Chronicon de Lanercost*, the *Scalacronica* of Sir Thomas Gray, Stevenson's *Documents Illustrative of the History of Scotland*, the *Anglo-Saxon Chronicle*, Raine's *Letters from the Northern Registers*, Palgrave's *Documents*, etc., *illustrating the History of Scotland*.

HERBERT MAXWELL.

MONREITH, *February*, 1911.

I

THE MAKING OF SCOTLAND AND THE QUESTION OF HOMAGE TO ENGLAND

A.D. 600—1290

I

THE liberality of an anonymous donor having put it in the power of the Governing Body of this University to establish a course of lectures on Scottish History, it is fitting that he who has been honoured with the privilege of opening that course, should be prepared with an answer to those (and they are not few in number) who question the utility of a knowledge of history to young men and women entering upon active life. Surely, I have heard it said, surely the past is over and done with; what concerns living men and women is the present and how to deal with it—the future and how to provide for it. Aye, but what more effective equipment can be had for dealing with human circumstance than an accurate knowledge of the events and individuals by whose agency the world and its separate nationalities have been evolved out of primitive and rigorous conditions and moulded into their present form and relations ?

I am often tempted to wish that our scheme of national education did not comprise so many subjects, and that after the elementary course is finished, more importance is not given to history, with which a sound acquaintance seems specially desirable in a country like ours, where, owing to a democratic franchise, the majority of schoolboys (not schoolgirls as yet, at all events) will exercise each his influence upon the future course of history through the parliamentary vote. In this matter I can speak from personal experience, for well I know that, when I entered parliament thirty years ago, a fuller knowledge than I possessed of past history would have enabled me to give better service during the six and twenty years that I sat there.

Now the best answer that can be given to those who regard a knowledge of history as an elegant superfluity was pronounced more than

INTRODUCTION

2000 years ago, when Thucydides dedicated his history of the Peloponnesian War to "those who desire to have a true view of what has happened, and of like or similar things which, *in accordance* with human nature (τὸ ἀνθρώπειον), will probably happen hereafter."

If that be admitted, then surely I need not urge the primary claim of the history of one's own country.

> Breathes there a man with soul so dead
> Who never to himself has said—
> This is my own, my native land?

Probably indifference to the land of one's birth is one of the rarest defects in human nature ; but patriotism, unless it is enlightened by a knowledge of what has gone before, is apt to assume a parochial cast. It is the function of history to raise the student's standpoint, to broaden his horizon, to enable him to read the past of his country and race in due relation to that of other nations. To fulfil this function it must be the right kind of history.

Now the vital part of history—the only part that really matters—is that which deals with the spirit and material condition of the people at various periods, the character and motives of their leaders, and the means through which they attained, or failed to attain, their ends. These are the points which I shall endeavour to keep before you in dealing with the period to be dealt with in this course—namely, the half century or thereby during which the Scots were continuously engaged in war to establish their national independence. I shall have to say some things which may offend the pre-possession of certain of my fellow-countrymen who hold that right was always and exclusively on one side, but I shall say them fearlessly, believing that when one undertakes to lay facts before those who lack leisure and opportunity to ascertain them for themselves, it is a crime against reason to tell anything short of the whole truth, so far as it can be known.

Before entering upon the story of the Scottish struggle for independence, I am afraid I must tax your patience by a brief recapitulation of the genesis of Scotland as a kingdom—how, in short, the people of Scotland came to be in a position to claim independence as a united nation.

In the eighth century, to go no further back, when Egbert was engaged with moderate success in consolidating the Saxon provinces into the realm of England, Northern Britain, then known as the land of Alba, was ranged mainly into four separate and mutually hostile kingdoms, namely: The Four Kingdoms of Alba, A.D. 700–800.

(1) The kingdom of Dalriada, founded as a Gaelic colony from Ireland by Fergus mor the son of Erc in the fifth century. These colonists were known as Scots, and although their territory included little more than Argyll, Lorn, and some of the adjacent islands, they ultimately gave their name to the whole of Northern Britain. Their capital or chief fortress was Dunadd, near the Crinan Canal, where there are many interesting remains.

(2) The kingdom of the Picts, extending north and east from Drumalban, the great central ridge of the Highlands. These Picts, be they a non-Arian race as Sir John Rhys would have us believe, or, as I venture to hold, a branch of the great Celtic migration which

7

overran Western Europe, appear to have dis-possessed an aboriginal race, of whom so little is known that we need not trouble ourselves about them here and now. The seat of the Pictish kings was at or near Inverness.

(3) The kingdom of Cumbria or Strathclyde, peopled by Britons, Cymri or, as we now call them, Welsh, a third branch of the great Celtic race. Its capital was Dunbarton = dun Bretann, the Britons' fortress.

(4) The Saxon kingdom of Bernicia or Nor-thumbria, extending from the Humber to the Firth of Forth, with a seat of government at Bamborough.

Besides these there was the province of Gallo-way where the Niduarian Picts had their native chiefs, who were subject alternately to Saxon, and later to Norse, dominion.

In 844 Kenneth MacAlpin, King of the Scots of Dalriada, having defeated the Picts by the help of the Danes, was crowned king over Alba, and his kingdom became officially termed Scotia or Scotland. But his rule only extended over central Scotland—Perthshire, Argyll, Angus

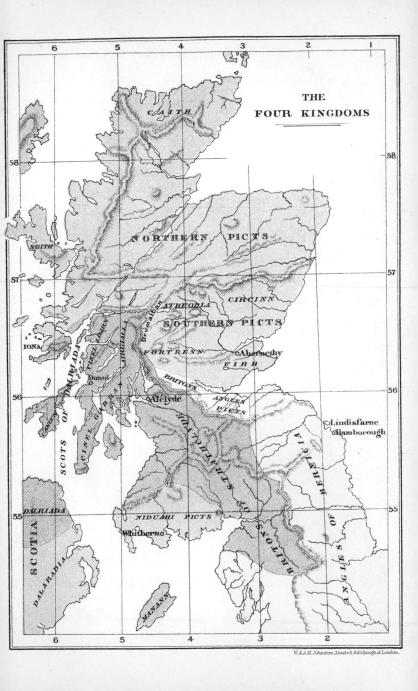

THE
FOUR KINGDOMS

6   5   4   3   2   1

58   58

CAITH

SGITH

57   57

NORTHERN   PICTS

ATHFODLA   *CIRCINN*

Dromalban   *SOUTHERN PICTS*

IONA   *FORTRENN*   o*Abernethy*

FIBH

DALRIADA   *Dunad* o

BRITONS

Alclyde   *ANGERS*
PICTS

SCOTS OF DALRIADA   *CINEL GABHRAN*   *CINEL LOAIRN*   *AIRGIALLA*

Lindisfarne
Bamborough

BRITONS OF STRATHCLYDE   *BERNICIA*

55   55

DALRIADA

NIDUARI   PICTS

SCOTIA   *Whitherno* o

DALARADIA   *ANGLES OF*

MANANN

6   5   4   3   2

W. & A.K. Johnston, Limited, Edinburgh & London.

and Mearns, and Fife. The Highlands proper —the ancient territory of the Picts, was partly held by independent Celtic (? Pictish) chiefs and partly by Norse settlers. Lothian, still nominally part of Northumbria, was alternately the prey of rival Saxon chiefs and the subject of Norse invasion. The Norse jarls of Orkney were beginning to establish their rule over Caithness, the Sudreys or Western Isles, Galloway and Man.

The work of consolidation proceeded slowly. It received a great impetus when Malcolm Ceann-mor, son of that Duncan whom Macbeth had slain, drove the usurper Macbeth across the Mounth, defeated and killed him at Lumphannan in Aberdeenshire. This was on 15th August, 1057, and I think you may reckon that as the real birthday of the kingdom of Scotland, albeit much remained to be done in reducing the outlying parts—Caithness, the Isles and Galloway—into subjection to the Crown.

Malcolm Ceann-mor, A.D. 1054– 1093.

Having brought this skeleton sketch thus far, I can no longer shirk the great question, long vexed, never yet settled, nor I think to be settled

The question of homage to England.

9

—was Malcolm Canmore, king of a wholly independent realm, or did he owe homage for part of his dominion to the Saxon King of England? The question might be settled off-hand if we could accept all extant documents as genuine; but one of the great perplexities which beset the student of early times is the frequency with which documents were forged. It was very easy to forge when not one man in a thousand could read or write. Now all men are agreed that the letter purporting to be from "Malcolm, King of Scots and the adjacent Isles," and his eldest son "Edward, Earl of Carrick and Rothsay," acknowledging that they held the kingdom of Scotland under their overlord, Edward the Confessor, and vowing fealty to him and his heirs, is a clumsy forgery, perpetrated by the notorious John Hardyng, who was employed in the fifteenth century by King Henry V. and Henry VI. to collect evidence in favour of the suzerainty of England over Scotland. Rymer found this document in the Chapter House at Westminster and printed it in his great work, the *Fœdera*.

THE QUESTION OF HOMAGE

It may be asked, how is it known to be a forgery? and if I pause to explain, the answer must suffice for several other forged documents bearing on the independence of Scotland.

First, King Malcolm is made to call himself King of the Isles, whereas the western isles were not ceded by Norway till 1266, just 200 years later than the alleged date of Malcolm's letter.

Second, King Malcolm is made to say that he was acting "with the assent and advice of his Queen Margaret, daughter of Edward the Confessor." Now Edward, to whom the letter purports to be addressed, died in 1066, and Malcolm did not marry Margaret till 1069.

Third, Malcolm's eldest son is called Earl of Carrick and Rothesay. There never was an earldom of Rothesay; but in 1398 David, eldest son of Robert III., was created Duke of Rothesay. As for the earldom of Carrick, that was never assumed for the heir-apparent of the crown until the days of Robert the Bruce, who inherited it from his Celtic mother in 1292.

The earliest assertion of the supremacy of the English monarch over Scotland occurs in the

Anglo-Saxon Chronicle, also known as the *English Chronicle*, a current journal of events carried down to the year 1154, of which seven copies have survived to our day. It contains the following entry for the year 924 :

"In this year ... King Eadward (the Elder) was chosen for father and lord by the King of Scots (Constantine II.) and the whole nation of the Scots, and Regnwald, and the son of Eadulf, and all those who dwell in Northumbria, as well English as Danes, and North-men and others, and also the King of the Strathclyde Welsh, and all the Strath-clyde Welsh."

It is upon this solitary record (which varies in details in the different copies of the *Chronicle*) that what is called the Great Commendation of Scotland rests, whereon, in after years, another King Edward, the first after the Conquest, mainly founded his claim to overlordship.

We come upon slightly firmer ground in the following reign. Constantine, King of Scots, re-signed in 944, and was succeeded by Malcolm I., to whom in the following year King Eadmund of England handed over the Welsh kingdom of Strathclyde on the tenure of faithful service in war.

THE QUESTION OF HOMAGE

It can hardly be questioned that this transaction was a measure of defence against the common and formidable enemy of the two kings—the Norsemen and Danes, who by this time had overrun the southern part of Strathclyde, represented by the modern counties of Cumberland and Westmorland, from their base in the Isle of Man.

Now, the contention of most Scottish historians has generally been that Eadmund made over Strathclyde to Malcolm in free gift as an inducement to or reward for active alliance against the Northmen. The English case was and is that it was a fief, constituting Malcolm and his successors vassals of the King of England. I confess I find great difficulty in differing from Mr. Freeman and Dr. Skene, both of whom regard the transaction as a hereditary fief implying vassalage. The *Saxon Chronicle*, taking it for what it may be worth for impartiality, records that when King Eadmund died in 946, the Scots "gave oaths" to his successor, King Eadred. Anyhow, fealty or no fealty, Malcolm remained in possession of Strathclyde, and the nature of the tenure by his successors was to be radically affected by the subsequent course of events.

We may pass more lightly over the homage alleged to have been exacted by King Eadgar for the cession of Lothian, the northern half of Northumbria, to Malcolm's son, Kenneth II., for the contemporary *Saxon Chronicle* does not mention it, and the claim rests upon a tract attributed to Simeon of Durham, who wrote at least 100 years after Lothian had been incorporated in the Scottish realm, probably by fair conquest.

Effect of the Norman Conquest upon Scotland, A.D. 1066.

Relations between the two kingdoms were profoundly affected by the Norman Conquest of England. The third and greatest of the four Malcolms—Ceann-mor, as he was called in Gaelic —was then on the Scottish throne. Edgar Ætheling, Saxon King-elect of England, took refuge at the court of Scone, and Malcolm married his sister Margaret, to whose grace and beauty all writers testify, and whose piety the church recognised by canonising her in 1250.

The Ætheling, as rightful claimant to the

crown of England, had strong support in Yorkshire and the north, and Malcolm actively
espoused his brother-in-law's cause. This
brought the terrible Conqueror down upon him.
King William invaded Scotland by sea and land
in 1072, exacting homage and taking hostages
from Malcolm at Abernethy. There need be
no question about the authenticity of the
statement by Florence of Worcester (a nearly
contemporary chronicle) that William exacted
homage from Malcolm at Abernethy, but for
what that homage was paid is of equal doubt
and importance. Did Malcolm III., as the
Anglo-Saxon Chronicle seems to imply, become
William's man and do homage for his whole
realm ? Or was it a renewal of the homage for
Strathclyde said to have been exacted from
Malcolm I. by Eadmund of England 130
years before ? Or was it merely the normal
homage due by Malcolm to William for twelve
English villæ or townships which, it appears,
William granted to him in order to secure
his alliance ? It would be quite according to
feudal practice that Malcolm should become

William the
Conqueror
invades
Scotland,
1072.

William's vassal for his English possessions, without in the least compromising the independence of his own kingdom. There was no regular system of taxation under feudal law; lands were held of the sovereign by knights who owed military service for them, sometimes paying a fee in money also. Edward I. paid homage to Philip III. for the lands he held from him in France; if our King George owned lands in France he could not be called on to pay homage to the President of the Republic, but he would be expected to pay the taxes leviable on his possessions, which are the modern equivalent of homage.

Malcolm III. invades England, A.D. 1088.

William the Conqueror having died in 1087, Malcolm promptly invaded England. William Rufus, with his brother Duke Robert, hastened out of Normandy, and moved against Malcolm with a fleet and an army. Most of his ships were lost, which may account for the pacific outcome of his interview with Malcolm when he met him in Lothian (*in provincia Loidis*). According to the *Anglo-Saxon Chronicle* Eadgar Ætheling and Duke Robert "mediated a peace between the kings, on condition that King Malcolm should repair to our king, and become his vassal, and in all the like subjection as to his father before him, and this he confirmed by oath. And King William promised him all the lands and possessions that he held under his father" (namely the 12 villæ and a subsidy of 12 gold marks annually), "but this lasted a short time only."

In 1093 William Rufus was very ill, and, as the *Anglo-Saxon Chronicle* informs us, "made many good promises of amendment, which, when he recovered, he was not diligent to perform." The same authority states that he had not performed his obligations to King Malcolm, and refused to receive him when, in obedience to William's summons, Malcolm repaired to Gloucester to meet him. Assuming that, under the treaty of Abernethy, homage was due by Malcolm for part of the Scottish kingdom, it is a fair question whether William's admitted breach of obligations to Malcolm did not void Malcolm's obligations to William, except those due for his English lands. Anyhow, Malcolm thought so, for he returned home in very ill humour, collected an army, invaded Northumberland and met his death near Alnwick, where his eldest son, Edward, perished also. The place they fell is still called Malcolm's Cross.[1] His next son, Duncan, had been given as a hostage under the treaty of Abernethy. William Rufus had liberated him on the death of the Conqueror, but Duncan had chosen to remain at the Norman court. Now, however, he hastened to Scotland to claim the throne, " having," says the *Anglo-Saxon Chronicle* " done such homage as King William required." Duncan is a fleeting and insignificant figure; but his brother Eadgar, who succeeded him in 1074, has been cited as having made full acknowledgment of William's overlordship, on the authority of two out of eight documents in the Durham Treasury purporting to be grants by Eadgar to various ecclesiastical bodies. Now, as I have said before, monks frequently made

[1] The original cross, of which only the stump now remains, having fallen into decay, a new cross was erected in 1774 by Elizabeth, Duchess of Northumberland.

use of what was nearly their monopoly of the art of writing to forge instruments to their own advantage. The *Lanercost Chronicle*, that frankest of contemporary records, teems with examples of fraud of that nature ; and two of these Durham charters must take rank among the grossest of such impostures. Take one of them as an example, a charter by King Eadgar to the Monks of Coldingham. It contains the statement that he is acting " under the license of William King of England, lord superior of the kingdom of Scotland."

Upon this charter Dr. Raine, who, as an Englishman, never showed himself unfavour-able to the English claim of suzerainty, pro-nounces as follows :

"It is a most palpable forgery, fabricated apparently for the express purpose of establishing the superiority of England. Never, perhaps, was there so miserable an attempt at imitation. The parchment, unlike that of the 11th century, is thin and imperfectly prepared ... every character-istic of the document belong to a period later by centuries than the reign of Edgar. But the seal gives the finishing stroke to the whole. It is, in fact, a bad imitation, upon a very reduced scale, of the great seal of Robert I. or Robert II. The name indicating the name of the king is broken away.... The charter is probably one of the alleged forgeries of Hardyng, the poetic chronicler, who lived in the reign of Henry VI., and received an annuity from the Crown for his services."[1]

It is to be noted that in the six undoubtedly genuine charters by Edgar, preserved at Durham, *there is no allusion whatever to the King of England ana his claim.*

It may occur to you that a claim which required to be supported by such nefarious devices was baseless from the first. I do not think that is so. I have already expressed my belief that the Norman kings found an existing obligation of homage to the English crown for the territory of Strathclyde; but we are approaching events which put the whole question upon a new footing.

David I.
A.D. 1124–1153.

In 1124 David, the youngest son of Malcolm Canmore and the saintly Margaret, succeeded to the Scottish throne. By this time the royal families of Scotland and England had been knit afresh by marriage ties. In 1100 Henry I. of England married Eadgith,

[1] Raine, *N. Durham*, Appendix viii.

20

sister of four successive Kings of Scots—
Duncan II., Eadgar, Alexander I., and David I.
King Henry changed his bride's name to
Maud, and she represented the Saxon blood
royal through her mother, Queen Margaret.
Alexander I. had also married Sibylla, a natural
daughter of Henry I. All this tended to
strengthen the English element in the Scots
realm ; a process which was greatly accelerated
when King David came to the throne in 1124.
He had passed his youth at the Anglo-
Norman court, where, as William of Malmes-
bury expresses it, " he was polished from the
rust of Scottish barbarity." By his marriage
with an English wife, daughter of Waltheof,
Earl of Northumberland, he received from
King Henry the Honour of Huntingdon, and
became thoroughly imbued with the doctrines
of feudalism. When he returned to Scotland
as king in 1124, he brought many young
Norman barons with him, granting them wide
lands in Moray and elsewhere. Among these
came one Robert de Brus, of whose descendants much more was to be heard, to whom

was granted the lordship of Annandale. You will perceive how the question of independence became complicated through these transactions. The greater part of the soil of Scotland was held in fief by Norman barons, who owed homage for their lands to the King of Scots; but the same barons owned lands in England, for which homage was due to the English crown.[1]

Feudalism established in Scotland.

The feudal system stinks in the nostrils of some of our modern constitutional writers, but it is my firm belief that it was the only system whereby David could have established his authority, so as to weld and hold together the diverse races that composed the people of

[1] At the present day, when the ancient titles of nobility have lost their significance, one bears to be reminded of the nature of feudal tenure. The monarch parcelled out those parts of his realm whereof he did not retain personal possession into large tracts, handing over the possession and governance of each to one of his principal knights, whom he created Count or Earl of the several county or earldom. In modern English we have retained the Saxon *eorl* to denote the dignity, and the term "county" from the French *comte* to denote the territory. The Earl in turn divided his earldom into baronies, each baron becoming his vassal, and further subdividing his land among knights and esquires, his sub-vassals.

Scotland. Think of it : David's subjects comprised the original Scots of Argyll and the Isles, with whom the northern Picts had become pretty well merged in the twelfth century; the Britons or Welsh of Strathclyde, dominated and largely expropriated by the English since King Eadmund's conquest in 945; the Saxon population of Lothian, the Picts of Galloway, and the fiery Norsemen who still kept their grip on Caithness and the Isles.

The motley character of David's subjects receives ample recognition in his charters. For instance, the original charter to the Abbey of Melrose in 1144 is addressed to "the Normans, English, Scots and Galwegians of the whole realm." Another in 1139 is addressed to Normans, English and Cumbrians, and so on, with many variations. When we remember that these various races had been constantly at war with each other for centuries, we recognise David's statesmanship in perceiving in the strong hand of feudalism the surest means of making them subject to the crown and uniting them in a spirit of common nationality.

The worst result of the system became apparent when King David invaded England in 1138 to support his niece Matilda in her conflict with Stephen. Several of his Norman barons found themselves in a dilemma; for if they refused to follow the King of Scots, their possessions in Scotland would be forfeited; whereas, if they marched with David, and failed to overthrow Stephen, they would lose their lands in England. Upon none of these did this double allegiance press more heavily than upon Robert de Brus, the friend of David's youth, to whom David had granted the lordship of Annandale in 1124.[1] Now de Brus had inherited from his father ninety manors, extending to 40,000 acres, in Yorkshire. He warned David of what would happen if he persisted in the expedition, reminding him that the Normans of his court were the best supporters of his throne, and that their defection would throw the realm into confusion. Failing to dissuade the king from his enterprise, de Brus renounced

[1] Robert I., King of Scots, was sixth in descent from this Robert de Brus.

his allegiance, resigned the lordship of Annandale, and joined King Stephen's army. His son,
another Robert de Brus, remained faithful to
David, and received the lands in Annandale.

The Scots were badly defeated at the battle of
the Standard, on Cowton Moor, near North-
allerton (22nd August, 1138); but as Northumberland and Cumberland were at that time
part of the Scottish realm, David escaped across
the border, and Stephen, having his own civil
war on hand, could not take advantage of his
victory, and allowed David to retain the Honour
of Huntingdon.

Battle of the
Standard,
22nd
August,
1138.

King David, dying in 1153, was succeeded by
his grandson Malcolm IV., the Maiden, who
was forced to surrender Cumberland and
Northumberland to Henry II., but indemnified
himself by the subjugation of Moray, where
the Celtic population had been strengthened by
a numerous settlement of Flemings. It was as
King Henry's vassal for the earldom of Huntingdon that Malcolm had to join the English
army in the campaign in France, whence he
was recalled in haste to put down a rebellion

Malcolm the
Maiden,
A.D. 1153–
1165.

in Galloway, and that turbulent province was finally incorporated in the realm.

William the Lion, 1165–1214.

We now come to a very momentous passage in the relation of the two kingdoms. William the Lion, King of Scots, succeeding in 1165; pressed Henry II. hard for the promised restoration of the earldom of Northumberland and the lordship of Cumberland. This Henry refused, but confirmed William in the Honour of Huntingdon, for which he did homage, and accompanied Henry as his vassal to the seat of war in France. Here the two monarchs fell out William opened negotiations with Louis VII., Henry's enemy, and thus laid the foundation of the Scoto-French league, which endured so long as Scotland remained a separate monarchy.

Treaty of Falaise, 8th December, 1174.

In the spring of 1174 William tried to wrest possession of Northumberland, but was taken prisoner and sent to Falaise in Normandy. He regained his liberty by agreeing to terms extorted from him by King Henry, whereby King William bound not only himself, but all his barons, to do homage to the King of England, giving up the castles of Roxburgh, Jedburgh,

Edinburgh, and Stirling as pledges, and many nobles and their sons as hostages. All ambiguity about the nature and scope of Scottish homage to England was at an end. King William and his barons did homage *for all that they had* to King Henry at York in August, 1175; and, had the treaty of Falaise been maintained, the independence of Scotland would have been a dream of the past. But that ignoble treaty was not maintained: it was revoked, cancelled, and utterly voided by King Richard Cœur de Lion in the treaty of Canterbury, 5th December, 1189. Richard, being sorely in want of cash for a crusade, accepted from William a sum, it is said, of 10,000 marks (about £100,000) in consideration for which he restored to William his castles, absolved him from all homage except for the earldom of Huntingdon, and surrendered all extant documentary evidence of the homage paid by King William and his barons at York. The bearing of this treaty of Canterbury is so important upon the future of Scottish independence that the exact terms, as preserved in Rymer's *Fœdera*, should be borne in mind :

Treaty of Canterbury, 5th December, 1189.

"We have rendered up to William, by the Grace of God King of Scots, his castles of Roxburgh and Berwick, to be possessed by him and his heirs for ever as their proper inheritance.

"Moreover we have granted to him an acquittance of all obligations which our good father, Henry, King of England extorted from him by new instruments in consequence of his captivity; under this condition only, that he shall completely and fully perform to us whatever his brother Malcolm, King of Scotland, of right performed, or ought of right to have performed, to our predecessors." [1]

The concluding sentence of this extract revives the old question as to the nature and extent of the homage due by Malcolm the Maiden. Was it for Strathclyde? Hardly, seeing that Henry II. had taken Cumberland and Westmorland, part of Strathclyde, away from Malcolm. It was probably only for William's English fiefs that homage was required; indeed William could not, according to feudal law and custom, have retained these valuable fiefs without rendering homage for them. One thing is perfectly clear, namely, that King William and his heirs were absolved from all claim on the part of the English king to homage

[1] *National MSS. of Scotland*, vol. i. no. 46.

n respect of the whole realm of Scotland, such
homage having been claimed and exacted for
the first time by Henry II. at Falaise. Yet
this was the claim that was afterwards revived
by Edward I.

Several times during the reign of King John Scottish
claim to
Northum-
berland.
(1199-1216) England and Scotland were on the
brink of war over the vexed question of the
ownership of Northumberland, to which William
never relinquished his claim. John had too
bitter a controversy on hand with his own
barons to let him willingly provoke a quarrel
with Scotland, though he secretly assisted the
Norse Jarl Harald, who was nominally King
William's vassal for Caithness, when he attempted to seize the province of Moray. John
does not take high rank among English statesmen, nevertheless there is some reason to reckon
him among the earliest to conceive and promote
the project of a peaceful union of the English
and Scottish crowns—a project which in succeeding centuries repeatedly presented itself to
thoughtful and far-seeing statesmen of both
realms as the natural destiny of the island of

Britain, and which was at length realised by the accession of James VI. to the English throne.

Alexander II.
A.D. 1214–1249.

Union of the crowns, or at least a close alliance, suggests itself as the motive underlying John's policy in securing from King William the marriage of Alexander, heir-apparent to the Scottish throne. It is true that King John had been dead five years when Alexander married his eldest daughter, Princess Joan, nor did the contract prevent King William, as an English baron, joining the other English barons in their rising against John, who retaliated by burning Berwick, the principal commercial port of Scotland. Moreover, the French Dauphin brought over some troops and made formal alliance with Alexander, but John's death in 1216 put an end to the war. In December, 1217, King Henry III. directed the sheriffs of Lincoln, Leicester, Cambridge, Huntington, Northampton, Rutland, Bedford, Buckingham, Essex, and Middlesex, to give seisin of the lands in these counties comprised in the Honour of Huntingdon to King Alexander, who had

returned to his allegiance (as an English baron).
Relations between King Alexander and his
brother-in-law, Henry III., continued on a good
footing, Alexander being engaged in the much
needed consolidation of his realm. The two
kings met at York on 25th September, 1237,
when Alexander released Henry from his promise to marry his sister Margery, resigned his
hereditary claim to the counties of Northumberland, Cumberland, and Westmorland, receiving
in consideration 200 librates of land in Northumberland for the annual rent of a soar hawk.
Alexander then renewed his homage and fealty
for his English possessions.

When Alexander III. succeeded his father in
1249 he was only eight years old. Two years
later he was knighted at York on Christmas
day by Henry III., to whose little daughter
Margaret he was married next day. King
Henry demanded of the bridegroom that he
should renew homage for his kingdom ; but
the boy had been too carefully warned against
falling into that trap. He said he must consult
his council before touching that matter. King

Alexander
III.
A.D. 1249–
1286.

Henry tried to persuade Pope Innocent IV. to grant an injunction against the coronation of the King of Scots, without consent of the King of England, whose vassal he was ; but the Pope declined to do so, whence it may be inferred that he recognised the independence of the kingdom of Scotland, which was not affected by the homage due for the Scottish king's English fiefs.

Consolidation of Scotland, 1263.

It was under Alexander III. that the realm of Scotland became what we know it to be now, minus Orkney and Shetland, and plus the Isle of Man. Alexander offered to buy the Western Isles from King Haco, who responded by appearing with a powerful fleet off the Isle of Skye, where he was joined by Magnus, Norse King of Man. Entering the Clyde late in September, 1263, Haco attempted to land at Largs, but he was repulsed, his ships were scattered by an autumn gale, and he retired to Kirkwall only to die. Three years later the Hebrides and the Isle of Man were annexed to the Scottish realm.

On the death of Henry III. in 1272, King

Alexander attended the coronation of his brother-in-law, Edward I. No homage appears to have been demanded, but in 1278 Alexander was summoned to London and tendered homage for his English fiefs, saving always his own kingdom. The Bishop of Norwich interrupted, saying, "And saving also the right of my lord Edward to homage for your kingdom." Alexander is said to have retorted—"That is due to God alone, for it is from Him only that I hold my crown."

Thereafter intercourse between the courts of England and Scotland continued politically harmonious and personally affectionate ; the friendship between these two wise and chivalrous monarchs seems to have laid to sleep the question of superiority. The untimely death of Alexander in 1286 must have been a national calamity in any case, for under his firm, temperate rule for thirty-seven years the country had reached a degree of prosperity without precedent. Well might Andrew of Wyntoun, father of Scottish history, lament in retrospect of a hundred years.

Death of Alexander III., 19th March, 1286.

> Quhen Alysander oure Kyng was dede
> That Scotland led in love and le,
> Away wes sons of ale and brede,
> Of wyne and wax, of gamyn and gle.
> Our gold wes changyd into lede ;
> Chryst, born into Virgynyté,
> Succoure Scotland, and remede
> That stad is in perplexité.[1]

Inter-
regnum,
1286–1292.
But the calamity was deepened a thousandfold
by the fact that Alexander died childless. His
two sons and his daughter Margaret, Queen of
Norway, had all been taken, and the succession
devolved upon Margaret's daughter, another
Margaret—a fleeting, pathetic figure whom
men styled the Maid of Norway. The succession had been settled upon her by the Parliament
of Scone in the year before Alexander's death
"failing any children that the king might have.'
Now this settlement obtained easy assent, seeing
that King Alexander, a hale man of forty-four
was just about to take a second wife, and was
not likely to die without surviving issue. But
when the succession was suddenly thrown open
by his death, strong objection was taken to

[1] *The Orygynale Cronykil of Scotland*, Book viii. ch. 2.

the accession of the Maid of Norway, or any woman, as being contrary to the ancient custom of Scotland. A regency of six guardians was appointed, consisting of William Fraser Bishop of St. Andrews, Duncan Earl of Fife, and Alexander Earl of Buchan, for the district north of the Firths; and for southern Scotland Robert Wishart Bishop of Glasgow, John Comyn Lord of Badenoch, and James the Steward. But another claimant to the throne appeared immediately. Robert de Brus, sixth Lord of Annandale, afterwards known as "the Competitor," was grand-nephew of William the Lion. In 1238 Alexander II., being then without male issue, acknowledged this lord as heir presumptive to the crown, which act was ratified by the Great Council, and was followed by the barons present doing fealty to de Brus. The birth of Alexander III. in 1241 extinguished de Brus's heirship; but when the male royal line failed with the death of Alexander III., de Brus took the field in arms to enforce his claim as heir male. It is significant that Fordun, Wyntoun, and Barbour, the only Scottish writers upon whom we can rely for the events of this period,[1] are silent upon the civil war raised by de Brus at this time. They all wrote after the line of Bruce was established on the throne, and discreetly suppressed the record of what might be to the discredit of the reigning house. But the publication of the Scottish Exchequer Rolls and other records amply demonstrate that Bruce and a number of other barons, including one of the guardians, James the Steward, did make war, seizing the castles of Dumfries, Buittle, and Wigtown, killing several men in assault upon the last-named place.

[1] None of the three was an actually contemporary writer. John of Fordun, probably a chantry priest at Aberdeen, collected material for his *Scotichronicon* and *Gesta Annalia* between 1364 and 1384 ; but the *Scotichronicon* was not made use of until Fordun had been dead about sixty years, when an anonymous compiler, reputed to be Walter Bower, Abbot of Inchcolm, took it in hand about 1440-47, and continued the chronicle down to the death of James I. John Barbour, Archdeacon of Aberdeen, was born about 1316, and Andrew of Wyntoun, Prior of Lochleven, was not born until about 1350. The material, other than oral tradition, upon which these writers worked, has entirely disappeared.

APPEAL OF GUARDIANS

In these perplexing circumstances, the Guardians of Scotland, within a fortnight of Alexander's death, sent envoys to ask advice of King Edward, presumably as the nearest relative of the infant queen.[1] Now, Mr. Andrew Lang has pointed out that if King Edward at this time believed he had any claim to the superiority of Scotland, he should have administered the country as his fief during the minority of Queen Margaret.[2] That he made no attempt to do so, seems fair proof that he had no intention of renewing a claim which he had abandoned during the life of his brother-in-law, Alexander III. A project of a different kind occupied his thoughts, one which Scottish partisans have cited as a proof of his selfish ambition, but which I wish to persuade you to regard as a wise and statesmanlike design. Scotland was threatened with—nay, was in the very throes of civil strife over the disputed succession : King Alexander's little grand-niece,

Guardians of Scotland appeal to Edward I., March, 1286.

[1] Stevenson's *Historical Documents*, i. 4. Original in Public Record Office.

[2] *History of Scotland*, vol. i. p. 170.

Margaret, when she should come from Norway, would have to fight her way to the throne. The happiest solution would be that the heir of England, Edward Prince of Wales, should marry Margaret Queen of Scotland, and so all matters of dispute between the two realms would be laid to rest for ever. To this project King Edward easily obtained the consent of King Eric of Norway; the Pope granted a dispensation for the marriage of the cousins-german; the Scottish guardians received the proposal with enthusiasm, and on 18th July, 1290, a treaty of marriage was concluded at Birgham.

Death of the Maid of Norway, Sept., 1290.

All this fair scheme was shattered by a calamity whereof one cannot speak without chagrin, even after the lapse of 600 years. On 7th October, 1290, the Bishop of St. Andrews informed King Edward that "there sounded through the people a sorrowful rumour that our lady was dead, on which account the kingdom of Scotland is disturbed." Rumour in this case was but too well founded. The Maid of Norway, who was probably not more

than eight years old, died on the voyage to
Scotland, and her body was landed in the
Orkneys.

There was widespread suspicion of foul play,
for it was against the interests of more than
one powerful baron of Scotland that the Maid
should be crowned. Barbour, whose theme
was the Bruce, makes no reference whatever to
Queen Margaret, but plainly declares that the
accession of a female to the throne was barred.
This was in accordance with the wishes of
Robert the Bruce himself, who in his charters
always represented himself as direct successor
to Alexander III., ignoring Queen Margaret
and King John Balliol altogether. Wyntoun,
on the other hand, has a purely fabulous
account of the Maid being put to death before
she left Norway, lest she should succeed to the
throne of that country.

In Norway the current belief was that she
had been kidnapped. Ten years later, in 1300,
a woman, native of Lubeck, gave out that she
was Margaret, Queen of Scotland, and persuaded so many people that she was so, that

when she was burnt as an impostor at Nordness in 1309, a church was erected on the site of her execution in memory of " the martyred Maritte."

There can be no reasonable doubt that Queen Margaret did die in or off Orkney, in the presence of Bishop Narve of Bergen, who took her remains back to Norway, where they were identified by her father, King Eric.

In the next lecture I will endeavour to show how the claim of English overlordship came to be revived.

II

INTERREGNUM, REIGN OF JOHN BALLIOL AND THE RISING UNDER WALLACE

A.D. 1290—1297

II

IN my last lecture I brought the narrative down to the autumn of 1290, when the untimely death of the Maid of Norway wrecked King Edward's fair project of uniting the crown of England and Scotland by the marriage of his son, Edward Prince of Wales, to the infant Queen of Scotland. I endeavoured to explain how the kings of the Celtic line, several of whom were sagacious statesmen, and all of whom were vigorous warriors, had forged four discordant nationalities into a single realm, and how they succeeded in doing so by introducing a fifth racial element—the feudal Norman barons. It will be my task to-night to endeavour to show how the political unity thus effected became inspired with a common national spirit through two agencies—(1) the aggressive attitude of the English government, and (2) the appearance of a capable patriotic leader, whose action was not hampered by the possession of lands in the English realm.

Since his accession in 1272, King Edward had never advanced any claim to superiority over Scotland, and had maintained most friendly relations with his brother-in-law, Alexander III. I am quite unable to share the unfavourable view expressed by some Scottish writers upon Edward's motives and designs down to this point. I believe that the whole trend of his policy towards the northern kingdom was pacific.

But the failure of the projected marriage, combined with the imminence of civil war between parties in Scotland, certainly brought about a change in his views, and he never was a man of half measures. I ask your attention to the important fact, too commonly overlooked, that Edward never interfered actively with the government of Scotland until he was invited to do so by *the leaders of both parties in the disputed succession*. On 7th October, 1290, Bishop William Fraser of St. Andrews, one of the four surviving Guardians of the realm, wrote to King Edward upon hearing of the death of Queen Margaret. His letter is remarkable as being the only extant contemporary document in which allusion occurs to an event of such supreme importance to Scotland as the death of her queen. Although it has often been printed, I must trouble you by quoting an extract from it :

Bishop Fraser's appeal to Edward I., 7th October, 1290.

"There sounded through the people a sorrowful rumour that our said Lady (Queen Margaret) was dead, on which account the kingdom of Scotland is disturbed. And the said rumour being heard and published, Sir Robert de Brus, who before did not intend to come to the said meeting,[1] came in great power to confer with some who were there ; but what he intends to do, or how to act, as yet we know not. But the Earls of Mar and Athol are collecting their army and some other nobles of the land are drawing to their party ; wherefore there is fear of a general war and a great slaughter, unless the Most High apply a speedy remedy through your exertion and good offices. . . . If Sir John de Balliol comes to your presence we advise you to take care so to treat with him that in any event your honour and advantage be preserved. If it turn out that our Lady hath departed this life (and may it not be so !) let your excellency

---

[1] A meeting of magnates summoned at Perth on 29th September to discuss the terms of the marriage with the English envoys.

deign if you please to approach towards the March for the consolation of the Scottish people, and to prevent the shedding of blood, so that the faithful men of the kingdom may keep their oath inviolate, and set over them for king him whom of right ought to have the succession, if so be that he will follow your counsel."

One writer has followed another in heaping obloquy on Bishop Fraser's memory as having betrayed the cause of Scotland in this letter. Has that obloquy been justly incurred? I venture to think that it has not. Fraser was one of the four surviving Guardians of Scotland; in fact he and John Comyn of Badenoch were conducting the government at this time; for James the Steward and, probably, Bishop Wishart of Glasgow, having been unfavourable to Queen Margaret's accession, had now espoused the cause of the Bruce. Fraser was desperately anxious to save his country from the misery of civil war; he perceived that Scotland stood in supreme need of some strong and, if possible, disinterested authority to protect her from the violence of her own barons. To whom could he appeal more hopefully than to the intimate friend and brother-in-law of the deceased King

Alexander ? Was the usually temperate Lord Hailes justified in denouncing Bishop Fraser's " dark and dangerous policy " and " his base proposal ? " The Bishop's allusion to " the faithful men of the kingdom keeping their oath inviolate " has always been interpreted as implying submission to the superiority of England ; but the only oaths we know of as having been previously received by King Edward were those of such barons as owned English fiefs. A fairer interpretation seems to be that the reference was to the allegiance due to the legitimate successor to Queen Margaret, implied in the oath of allegiance to King Alexander, " his heirs and successors." The sole passage in this celebrated letter which supports the charge of underhand dealing is the reference to the choice of a king " who will follow your counsel."

Now Bishop Fraser and the legitimists were not the only party invoking the counsel of King Edward at this time. Before the end of the year he received an appeal from the opposition, to wit—the Seven Earls of

Scotland, who, claiming to speak in the name
of the community, lodged protest against the
conduct of the two guardians, alleged an ancient
right vested in the Seven Earls to elect the
King of Scotland and indicated Robert de Brus
of Annandale as the rightful heir under the
settlement of Alexander II. in 1238.[1]

Seeing, then, that both the Guardians and
the Seven Earls—representing Government and
Opposition—had invoked the interference of
their powerful neighbour, is King Edward to
be suspected of sinister design because he took
up the question seriously? No doubt there
were men in his council—the Bishop of Norwich, for instance—who had never relinquished
the idea of the overlordship, and who would
seize this fresh opportunity for pressing it.
Nay, the very action of both great parties in
Scotland in referring the question of the succession to King Edward, seemed to imply a
national recognition of his moral, if not legal,
superiority; and King Edward, thus prompted,
was not slow to adopt the views of his advisers.

[1] Palgrave's *Documents and Records*, pp. 14-23.

Sorrowfully, indignantly if you like, we must admit that the revival of the claim of suzerainty was brought about by the dissensions of the Scottish barons among themselves. There even exists a letter from one of the competitors for the crown, unsigned, but almost certainly Robert de Brus the Elder, arguing that Richard I. had exceeded his powers in releasing the homage of Scotland, and craving King Edward's support for the writer as claimant to the crown.

The contemporary English chronicler, Walter of Hemingburgh, describes the invitation to King Edward as a national act on the part of the Scottish people, to which Lord Hailes takes objection, saying that he saw "no sufficient evidence that the act was *national*," although many of the nobles may have invited the intervention of England. Seeing, however, that not only the Scottish guardians, but the pre-feudal constitutional body of the Seven Earls, independently appealed to the same authority, their action seems to have been as "national" as the constitution of the nation admitted. It is easy to talk about the general consent of a nation, but it is no more than a phrase when applied to a nation composed of such dissimilar races—Gaels, Welsh, Saxons, and Normans—as Scotland was in the thirteenth century. The commonalty enjoyed no means of expressing their views, except through the prelates and barons composing the estates, who were deeply divided on the question of the succession ; unanimous only in appealing to King Edward to settle it. The national will, therefore, was interpreted by the voice of a narrow, and chiefly alien, oligarchy.

Edward's beloved Queen Eleanor died only a few weeks after Queen Margaret. So soon as Edward had attended to her obsequies, he gave attention to the problem submitted to him. His first act was to cause search to be made through the documents in the English monasteries for evidence as to the former relations between England and Scotland. His second act was to respond to Bishop Fraser's request by warning his northern barons to muster at Norham on 3rd June, each with his proper contingent of horse and foot. That was the ordinary feudal method of mobilisation. His third act was to invite the Scottish prelates and barons to confer with him at Norham on 10th May. By this arrangement of dates, should the conference end unsatisfactorily or come to naught, the king would have his army ready to enforce his decree. For by this time he had determined to arbitrate only as Lord Paramount, and unless he were accepted as such he would not trouble his head to avert war, civil or otherwise, from a nation which could not settle its own affairs.

The conference on 10th May was opened by the king's speech, composed for him in Latin by the Provincial of Preaching Friars, and delivered *in French*[1] by the Justiciar of England.

International Conference at Norham, May, 1291.

[1] French continued to be the official language of the King of England's court and of the Law Courts until the reign of Edward III. It is not quite extinct yet. Every Act of Parliament receives the Royal assent in the word pronounced by the Clerk of the House of Lords : " Le Roi le veult." In the Irish courts French lingered long ; it is amusing to mark how naively English terms were used to supplement lapses of memory on the part of the clerks. Thus in the seventeenth century a case is recorded in

INTERREGNUM

It announced that the king accepted the office
of arbitrator out of good-will and affection to
the whole nation, being himself interested in its
safety, and he demanded, as a preliminary, that
the Scottish representatives should acknowledge
him as Superior and Lord Paramount.

The Scots plenipotentiaries requested time
to consider such a momentous demand : they
were given twenty-four hours. Next day they
asked for further delay. King Edward gave
them three weeks, by which time his army
would be assembled at Norham; and two, at
least, of the competitors for the Scottish crown,
namely Robert de Brus and John de Balliol,
were summoned as Edward's lieges, to attend
with their armed contingents.

At the preliminary conference were read all
the extracts collected out of the manuscript
records which could be held to prove the
performance of homage by Scottish kings.
These need not occupy our attention at this
day; because, however sincere King Edward's

Dyer's *Reports* of a prisoner who, after receiving sentence,
"ject un brickbat a le justice, que narrowly mist."

intention may have been in ordering them to be produced, we, knowing how easily and unscrupulously documents were forged to serve special interests in an age when very few laymen could read or write, must view that kind of evidence with the utmost suspicion. The treaty of Falaise was produced, of course, showing how William the Lion surrendered the independence of his kingdom to Henry II.; but the treaty of Canterbury, whereby Richard Cœur de Lion restored that independence, received no mention!

The conference reassembled at Upsettlington, on Scottish soil, on 2nd June. There were then nine competitors for the crown of Scotland, of whom all were present, except John de Balliol, who mistook the day. The Bishop of Bath recited the proceedings at the former conference, and, referring to the historical researches undertaken by command of King Edward, declared that it was quite clear that the kings of England had been Lords Paramount of Scotland from the most distant ages. Had the Scots any evidence to the contrary?

Adjourned to Upsettlington, 2nd June, 1291.

53

If so, let them produce it at once, and the king would be convinced by it if it was stronger than his own. Then the competitors present were asked to declare severally that they acknowledged Edward as Lord Paramount of Scotland, and would accept him as arbiter in the disputed succession. Robert de Brus (not he who was afterwards king of Scots, but his grandfather) was the first to reply, and he gave his assent "definitely, expressly, publicly and openly." All the rest followed in the same avowal, Balliol appearing next day and doing likewise.

The English chancellor then announced that, although King Edward had established his claim to the superiority of Scotland, he must not be held to have relinquished his rights of property in that realm, which might be claimed hereafter at a fit time. This claim may have referred only to the provinces of Lothian and Strathclyde; but it was dangerously vague and ambiguous. Anyhow the nine competitors, every one of whom were Norman barons, set their seals to the following acknowledgment:

SUBMISSION OF COMPETITORS

"Forasmuch as the King of England has evidently shown to us that the sovereign seignory of Scotland and the right of determining our several pretensions, belong to him, we, therefore, of our own free will and without compulsion, have agreed to receive judgment from him as our Lord Paramount, and we become bound to submit to his award."

On the following day, 4th June, the nine competitors consented to surrender the kingdom of Scotland and its castles to King Edward, on the pretext that, as the bestowal of the kingdom had been committed to him, he could not bestow that which he did not actually possess. This was formally carried out on 11th June. A hazardous transaction, one should say, from a Scottish point of view; but it is clear that Edward did not at this time entertain any sinister design of annexation, because, although it had been agreed that he was to hold the kingdom and castles for the space of two months after he had given his award, in fact he restored the kingdom to the four guardians and the castles to their keepers on the very day on which they were surrendered—namely, 11th June.[1]   The king

[1] Bain's *Calendar*, ii. 496.

did not pronounce his award till 17th November, 1292, seventeen months later.

On 12th June the Scottish prelates and barons presented Alan, Bishop of Caithness, to King Edward, who appointed him Chancellor of Scotland, with his own clerk, Sir Walter de Amundesham, as colleague. Also, on the 13th, he appointed Brian Fitz Alan as an associate with the four guardians, who now held their commission as regents from the King of England as overlord. These regents, with twenty-seven other earls and barons of Scotland, then swore fealty to Edward on the Holy Gospels.

One point remains obscure in these proceedings—how far did the acts of these Scottish prelates and barons commit the community—the people of Scotland ? It is expressly mentioned in the instruments attesting the proceedings at Upsettlington that they took place in presence of the clergy, nobles and *community* of Scotland. The four guardians, the prelates, the competitors and the other barons present assented to every part of the proceedings, admitting

SIR JOHN DE BALLIOL

Edward's claim in full. Did the representatives of the community—the *probi homines* or freeholders—silently consent also? Apparently not, for although no mention of them appears in the official version of the Great Roll given in Rymer's *Fœdera*, the copy of that Roll in the chronicle of St. Albans bears the statement that a written reply to Edward's claim was put in by the community, but that it was of no effect. Probably it was allowed "to lie on the table," as we should express it in modern procedure. Anyhow, in this chance admission by the St. Albans' chronicler we catch the first glimpse of the patriot feeling of united Scotland, shadowy enough at first, but soon to be so inspired by the fiery genius of Wallace as to draw into its vortex those very barons who had just signed away the independence of their country.

Now, I am not going to weary you by going further into the lengthy proceedings which ended on 17th November, 1292, by King Edward, naming Sir John de Balliol rightful heir to the crown of Scotland. By

Crown awarded to John Balliol, 17th November, 1292.

that time the number of competitors had risen from nine to thirteen, and it is to be noted that, so complete was the Norman ascendency in the ancient land of the Pict, the Gael and the Cumbrian, that although all these thirteen competitors claimed in virtue of their descent from daughters or sisters of Scottish kings (except Eric, King of Norway, who founded upon being the father of the deceased Queen Margaret), only one, Patrick Galythly, was a native Scot. What I wish you to note is that nothing could be more formal or complete than the absolute renunciation of Scottish independence which the competitors, the four guardians, and the other prelates and barons present, had made in the name of the Scottish people.

It is a bitter thing for a Scotsman, even at this distance of time, to have to admit that his country was delivered into dependence by the act of her own statesmen, of whom such as were laymen were mostly Edward's lieges for lands in England. Dissension and mutual jealousy among them left them with no alternative but submission or civil war.

GROUNDS OF AWARD

One thing is to be remembered : so far as we can gather from the scanty records, the fierce detestation of Edward of England, which generations of Scotsmen have been trained to cherish, had no existence at the time of the settlement. That arose out of what followed. Hitherto King Edward had been looked upon, not as an aggressive tyrant, but as a powerful friend of the Scottish court, nearly related in blood to the lost line of Malcolm Ceann-mor, and the most likely authority to effect a peaceable settlement of the succession. That he should exact acknowledgment of his overlordship was the fee for his services as arbitrator ; to be regretted, no doubt, but preferable to the terrible and bloody confusion which it averted. If these conditions be lost sight of, no clear view can be had of the course of events, the motives of the chief actors therein, or the general temper of the Scottish people.

Before passing forward to the brief reign of King John Balliol, a moment's consideration may be given to the grounds upon which King Edward preferred John's claim to that of his

Grounds of the award.

only formidable rival. John de Balliol claimed as the son of Devorguila, daughter of Margaret, *eldest* daughter of David, Earl of Huntingdon, youngest brother of King Malcolm the Maiden and King William the Lion. He was, therefore, great-grandson of the Earl of Huntingdon, and great-grand-nephew of two kings of Scots.

Robert de Brus claimed as son of Isabella, *second* daughter of the said Earl of Huntingdon ; he was, therefore, grandson of the Earl and grand-nephew of the two kings.

The question had not been previously decided in feudal law whether the succession should devolve on the person *second* in descent from the *elder* sister (Balliol), or *first* in descent from the *younger* sister (Bruce). So completely had Scotland become feudalised that, although the question involved was one of descent from her Celtic monarchy, the ancient Celtic law of Tanistry does not seem to have been so much as mentioned. Under that law, succession went by descent from a common ancestor, but choice had to be made by the people of a man of full age, fit for war and council, instead of the infant son or grandson of the last king.

King Edward's decision in favour of Balliol was in accordance with the modern interpretation of primogeniture, and de Bruce raised no objection to it, although he had in his favour the act of Alexander II., who, in 1238, under the law of Tanistry, had presented de Brus to his council as heir to the throne, and caused all present, clerics and laymen, to take the oath of fealty to him on the Holy Gospels.

De Brus was a very old man in 1292, else he might not have accepted Edward's award so patiently; but he had a grandson who bore these things in mind, and acted upon them when an opportunity arose.

On 19th November, 1292, the kingdom and castles of Scotland were handed over to King John Balliol. Next day he did homage and fealty to King Edward; the Great Seal of the Guardians was broken and the fragments deposited in the English treasury in token of the superiority of England. The first use King

King John does homage for his realm, 20th November, 1292.

John made of his new seal was to append it to letters patent, written from Newcastle-on-Tyne on Christmas Eve, announcing to the Scottish people that he had done homage to King Edward for his kingdom. Immediately afterwards, he executed a deed releasing King Edward from all the promises he had made and obligations undertaken while Scotland was under his governance. This was a serious act, as King John was soon to find. Under the treaty of Birgham it was expressly stipulated that no military aid was to be claimed by the King of England, and that no Scottish lawsuit should be appealed to an English court. Now a certain Gascon merchant had a " ganging plea " against the King of Scots for payment of £2197 due for wine supplied to Alexander III. Failing to get justice in Scottish courts, he carried his appeal to Westminster. King Edward summoned King John to appear in person at Westminster and answer the claim.

From this time forward Edward's whole policy towards the Scottish king and nation underwent a change. He was on the point of going to war with Philip of France, having refused to attend his court as vassal for his French possessions and having formally renounced his homage. This state of matters naturally would have caused him, as a matter of ordinary prudence, to keep on friendly terms with the Scots ; but, unfortunately, it came to his knowledge that John was secretly negotiating with King Philip for an offensive and defensive alliance against the Kings of England and Germany. To put a stop to that, on 29th June, 1294, he summoned King John and eighteen Scottish barons with their forces to join him as their overlord on 1st September in London for the French war. The Scottish king and nation had been specially exempted by the treaty of Birgham from military service in English armies, but John was playing traitor, which King Edward held to void all agreements. John had attended Edward's parliament in May, and, according to the English chronicler Hemingburgh, promised military aid, but when the summons came in the following month, he paid no attention to it.

Edward's hands were too full with his campaigns in Wales and France to allow him immediately to enforce his authority in Scotland.

King John renounces his homage, October, 1295.

It was not until October, 1295, that he received letters in which King John formally renounced his homage, informed him of the terms of his treaty with King Philip, and announced that his son, Edward Balliol, was to marry King Philip's niece.

This renunciation by King John was the one courageous act of his life. It involved him in perjury, to be sure; but had not King Edward, whose stern maxim was *Pactum serva !* done the like in renouncing his homage to Philip of France. In making his renunciation, John declared that his homage had been extorted by violence, which could only refer to the presence of the English army during the proceedings at Upsettlington. A weak, unwarlike spirit, John in reclaiming his independence no doubt was acting under strong pressure from Buchan and other barons.

Both nations now prepared for war. Edward assembled an army at Newcastle and forfeited all the English possessions of Scottish barons who would not repair to his banner. Robert de Brus, the competitor, was dead, but his son, father of the future king of Scots, was Edward's governor of Carlisle, and it fell to his lot to strike the first blow for the monarch whose decision had shut him out from succession to the Scottish throne. Balliol's army, under John Comyn, Earl of Buchan, invaded Cumberland on 26th March, 1296, invested Carlisle on the 28th, but, being repulsed, made a bloody raid on Tynedale, burning Hexham and Corbridge, and, if we can believe a notarial instrument afterwards drawn up for King Edward, perpetrated horrid cruelty upon the people. Herodian barbarities are said to have been committed on women, and two hundred " little clerks " were burnt in the church school at Corbridge. This was in the second week of April, and may possibly have been in reprisal for a massacre inflicted by King Edward on the people of Berwick, on 29th and 30th March. These events demand more than passing notice, for two reasons—first, because they marked the

War of Independence begins, March, 1296.

E
65

outbreak of the war of independence, and second, because in the course of 250 years following, though there was plenty of hard fighting, there occurred no single instance of similar brutalities on the part of the Scots.

The sack of Berwick, 29th and 30th March, 1296.

The sack of Berwick was an awful affair, and remains the darkest stain on the chivalrous memory of Edward I. He crossed the Tweed below Coldstream on 28th March, while the warlike Antony Bek, Bishop of Durham, led another column across at Norham. The English fleet attacked the town prematurely, and was repulsed with the loss of four ships that grounded in the river and were burnt by the Scots. Edward summoned the town and gave twenty-four hours for an answer. The immediate reply was a taunting refusal. The assault was delivered on Good Friday; the walls being weak and low were easily stormed, but King Edward's favourite kinsman, a brother of the Earl of Cornwall, was killed in the fray, upon which Edward fell into a frenzy and gave the order " No quarter !" A frightful massacre then began and lasted for two days. Wyntoun says that it came to an end only because Edward himself saw a woman in the act of childbirth being put to the sword. At this dreadful sight he turned away crying " *Laissez, laissez !* "

Berwick was at that time the chief commercial port of Scotland, and the Flemish merchants had a strong building there called Aula Rubra or Red Hall. Being bound by their charter to hold this to the last against the English, right well did thirty gallant fellows fulfil their engagement. They held out till evensong, after the town was taken, when the Red Hall was fired and the defenders all perished in the flames. The Scottish chronicler, Wyntoun, and the English, Walter of Hemingburgh, agree in estimating the total death roll at between 7000 and 8000 of all ages and both sexes. The Lanercost chronicler, an eye-witness, reckoned it at 15,000. Any women and children who survived were sent into perpetual exile, and the good town was ruined for ever.

The town had been taken, but the castle still frowned defiance from the height now occupied by the railway station. Commander of the

garrison was Sir William Douglas, well-named
"Le Hardi," the first illustrious chief of a
house that, in time coming, was so powerfully
to sway the destiny of Scotland for good or ill.
The place was strong : King Edward, burning
to set forward into Scotland, would not give the
time needful to reduce it.   He offered terms,
which were accepted ; the garrison to go free
on perpetual parole, only Douglas to remain
a prisoner ; for alas ! had not Douglas sworn
fealty to Edward in person as overlord of
Scotland ?

In all our land I know of no scene more
tranquil—none more deeply charged with
solemn memories—than the ample prospect that
lies before one standing on the height above
Tweedmouth.   The stately river sliding silently
seaward as of yore—the German Ocean launch-
ing leisurely rollers on the strand—the spacious
firmament o'erhead, sullied by no grimy waste
of industry—all these seem to breathe only
peace and security.   Yet each has the same grim
story for the understanding ear—the story of
that direful Good Friday when there rose from

the unhappy town the long din of butchery—
hoarse shouting of men, shrill screams of women
and wailing children ; and every gutter became
a tributary of Scottish blood to the Tweed.

If Edward calculated upon striking terror
among those whom he regarded as rebellious
subjects by this display of inhuman cruelty,
never was a ruler further out in his reckoning.
He lived to learn the lesson which many of his
successors had to lay to heart—that Scotsmen
may be led—they may, alas, be bribed—but
they will never be driven.

But patriot Scots had yet a while to wait for
a capable leader. Balliol's cause was lost at
Dunbar, where, on 28th April, the Earl of
Warenne completely routed his forces under
Comyn, Earl of Buchan. The Scottish historian,
Fordun, attributes the defeat to the defection
of the Earls of Mar and Athol, who, he says,
" through good will and love for Bruce," left
the field without striking a blow. This can
hardly have been true about Athol, who was
taken prisoner and sent to the Tower of London.
The competitor's son, Robert Bruce le viel,

King John's
defeat at
Dunbar,
28th April,
1296.

was, as we know, Edward's governor of Carlisle at this time. Fordun avers that his allegiance had been secured by a promise of the Scottish throne so soon as Balliol should be disposed of ; but that when Bruce claimed this promise after the battle of Dunbar, Edward exclaimed testily : "Ne avonis ren autres chose à fer que à vous reaymis ganere ?"—"Have we nothing else to do but win realms for you ?" Meanwhile, King Edward understood how to play off the Bruce party against the Balliols ?

Had the Scottish barons and people been united, they might have set Edward at defiance, so hampered was he by his French war and by the rebellion in Wales. But he induced James the Steward, a strong partisan of Bruce, to surrender Roxburgh Castle on 13th May, and to swear on the gospels (as usual) to aid him against John de Balliol, late King of Scotland. What chance, then, had the Scottish people of repelling invasion, having civil war in their midst ? Well might chronicler Fordun exclaim —"Woe is me ! through this quarrel the innocent populace lay mangled far and wide over the land, defenceless against the ravening of these wolves."

Having destroyed Berwick, Edward led his forces through Scotland, as far north as Elgin, meeting with no opposition and receiving the homage of all landowners. King John, perceiving the game was up, formally abdicated on 7th July, 1296, having reigned three years and seven months, handing to Antony Bek, Bishop of Durham, the resignation of his crown and people, together with his royal seal. Returning to Berwick in August, King Edward held a parliament, inspected and completed the famous Ragman Roll, which he had left there to be sworn to and signed. By this document nearly two thousand Scottish barons, knights and ecclesiastics, swore fealty on the gospels to the King of England, and renounced the league with France. In that roll is to be found, I think, the name of almost every individual of full age who afterwards distinguished himself on the Scottish side in the war of independence, with the notable exception of two—to wit, William Wallace and James of Douglas.

Abdication of King John, 7th July, 1296.

The names of James the Steward, progenitor of the Stuart dynasty, Robert de Brus le viel, and that younger Robert, the future king, appear among a host of others who had no scruples about breaking these solemn oaths when promising opportunity arose. One of the strangest phenomena of thirteenth century politics was the value attached by statesmen to the oaths of those whom they wished to secure, notwithstanding that reiterated experience proved that such oaths bound nobody. The only advantage was that the exaction of an oath enabled King Edward to hang as traitors those who broke it—when he could catch them.

In October King Edward, feeling satisfied that Scotland was under his heel, appointed the Earl of Warenne (afterwards of Surrey) as his warden, and left for London, taking with him three coffers containing the Scottish records, the Black Rood of Scotland, and the Stone of Destiny from Scone. In carrying off this stone to Westminster, King Edward no doubt had in mind the ancient prophecy that wherever the

Removal of the Stone of Destiny, 1296.

72

Stone of Destiny should be, there the monarchy of Scotland would be also. And so it has turned out, but not exactly in the sense that Edward attached to it.

No sooner was King Edward's back turned than the national spirit began to give trouble in Scotland. We can easily imagine that the English officers and garrisons, who had been left to administer the government and enforce the laws, were neither tactful nor considerate in their dealings with a conquered people. Anyhow, there was some kind of rising during the winter of 1296-7, for in January orders were issued that no man, cleric or layman, was to be allowed to leave Scotland. Probably William Wallace was the chief mover in the disturbance; but very little is known of the early days of our national hero, though much has been reported. His biographer, Blind Harry, lived two centuries later, and his ballad is a mere rehearsal of oral tradition, coloured by intense hatred of everything English. Walter Bower, working upon Fordun's notes a hundred years after Wallace had won immortal renown, states that " although

William Wallace, 1272 (?) –1305.

73

among the earls of the realm and the nobles he was considered as of mean degree, yet his forefathers were distinguished by knighthood. Also his elder brother was girt with the knightly belt, and owned a patrimony in landed estate large enough for his station, which he left to his descendants."

It is usually believed that William was a younger son of Malcolm le Waleys of Ellerslie, near Paisley, and that he got into trouble through youthful irregularities. Ellerslie being in Strathclyde, that is ancient Cumbria, it would appear from the name le Waleys, which means the Welshman, that the family was of the old British or Welsh nationality, who managed to retain their possessions when the Saxon king, Edward the Elder, conquered Strathclyde in 924.[1]

There is no doubt, I think, that William Wallace was a fugitive from justice in the winter of 1296-7. Blind Harry's story is that, when William was at school in Dundee, the English

[1] There are four signatories of the Ragman Roll named le Waleys, three from Ayrshire and one from Berwick.

governor, Selby, seeing the lad dressed in a fine suit of green, asked him how he dared to wear "so gay a weed," and tried to take his knife from him, whereupon Wallace "stiket him to the dead." Such a crime, had it occurred, is not likely to have escaped notice by English chroniclers, and the death of Governor Selby would have been officially recorded. There is no mention of the incident anywhere, except by Blind Harry; and I incline to trace Wallace's outlawry to another and less romantic source. When King Edward was at Perth on 8th August, 1296, the gaol delivery notes that a certain priest, Matthew of York, was accused of entering a woman's house in company with one William le Waleys, and stealing 3s. worth of beer. Matthew claimed benefit of clergy (that is, to be dealt with by the ecclesiastical courts), and Waleys had decamped.[1]

A fugitive from justice, whatever may have been the nature of his offence, Wallace would readily join in any action of disaffected Scots. Prominent among the movers of revolt were

[1] Bain's *Calendar*, ii. no. 185.

James the Steward, Bishop Wishart of Glasgow, Sir Andrew de Moray, and Sir William Douglas le Hardi, all of whom were Edward's sworn lieges, uneasy in their consciences, therefore, and requiring some more fiery spirit to confirm their counsels. Such a spirit came among them in the person of young Wallace. Bower describes how he prevailed over these great men by sheer force of will and courageous purpose.

Robert de Brus, Earl of Carrick, 1274-1329.

And now we come to the first appearance in history of Robert the Bruce, young Earl of Carrick, and a remarkable appearance it is. His father, Robert le viel, was still governor of Carlisle, whither young Robert, being then in his twenty-third year, was summoned, and made to swear on the consecrated host and the sword of Becket that he would do faithful and vigilant service to King Edward. He was then sent to quell the insurrection in Lanarkshire, and made a raid upon the lands of Douglas ; but, coming within the sphere of Wallace's influence, he speedily repented, and joined the patriots, making the usual excuse that his oath had been extorted from him by force.

ROBERT THE BRUCE

The insurrection rapidly gained strength, but jealousy among its leaders brought it to nought. Wallace appears to have been working for the restoration of the Balliol king ; probably Moray was also ; but neither Bruce, James the Steward nor Douglas can have had any such design. The Scottish force lay encamped at Irvine in the beginning of July, awaiting attack by Percy and de Clifford. Sir Richard de Lundin was so disgusted with the state of matters that he went over to the English, declaring he would not have more to do with men who could not agree among themselves. The result was the humiliating capitulation of Irvine, whereat Brus, the Steward, Douglas, Lindsey, Bishop Wishart and the rest submitted to King Edward's grace, making abject confession of " arson, homicide and various robberies" committed within his lordship in the land of Scotland and Galloway and agreeing to undergo what penalty he might decree.

Capitulation of Irvine, July, 1297.

Wallace the Landless bore no part in this submission. Leaving his wealthy colleagues to make their own terms, he rode off with all who would follow him into Selkirk forest.

RISING UNDER WALLACE

In August King Edward sailed for Flanders taking with him a great number of the Scottish knights captured at Dunbar, who now willingly exchanged prison walls for active service against the French, without inquiring over nicely into the justice of King Edward's quarrel with Philip. Wallace and young Andrew de Moray had gone to the north of Scotland, where, being rid of Norman barons trembling for their English possessions, they gathered a powerful force of humbler folk, and gave the rising a thoroughly national and popular character.

This was the secret of Wallace's greatness; he united intuitive military skill with the gift of bending other and older men to his will. The extraordinary effect of this ascendency was that, within two months of the capitulation of Irvine, where the patriot cause seemed to be utterly wrecked, Wallace was in command of a force which enabled him to lay effective siege to Dundee Castle. But he had to raise the siege on hearing that the Earl of Surrey was marching north in great strength. Wallace drew off to meet him, occupying the north bank of the

Forth opposite Stirling. Surrey was in ill humour, for he had been under orders for the French campaign, where there was good prospect of capturing valuable prisoners, when he received fresh orders to remain in Scotland to hold Wallace in check. Small prospect of gain from ransom in that quarter, the Scots having been deserted by all men who had any property at stake.

Surrey, finding the Scots so strongly posted, tried first to come to terms with them by means of two friars; but Wallace declined to treat. His troops lay on and about the Abbey Craig, so conspicuous at this day among other heights from the Wallace Monument erected in 1861. There was a long wooden bridge across the Forth, perhaps about where the older of the two stone bridges now stands, but more probably at a ford lower down, where the river runs nearest to the Abbey Craig. Surrey ordered his advanced guard to cross the bridge, under command of Sir Hugh de Cressingham, Edward's Treasurer of Scotland, Sir Marmaduke de Twenge commanding the cavalry. Sir Richard de Lundin, the same who deserted

Battle of Stirling Bridge, September, 1297.

the Scot's camp at Irvine, strongly demurred to these tactics, offering to show the way over a ford, whereby the Scots might be outflanked. But Surrey, despising the raw levies opposed to him, would not listen to this advice; perhaps he distrusted Lundin as a recent recruit. The bridge was so narrow that only two horsemen could ride over it abreast. It was midday before Cressingham's column formed up on the north side. It is no slight proof of Wallace's power of discipline that he allowed the whole column to file across before he gave the signal for attack. But his time had now come. Sending flanking parties along the river banks, he fell upon the English front in superior numbers and with so fierce an onslaught as to throw the enemy into dire confusion. Retreat across the narrow bridge was impossible. Sir Thomas Gray, in his soldierly narrative, says that Wallace had broken it down so soon as the English advanced guard had crossed. There was a great slaughter; probably few of Cressingham's men escaped, he himself being slain, and, according to the English chronicler, Hemingburgh, he was flayed and his skin made into saddle-girths, *erat enim pulcher et grossus nimis*— "for he was a handsome man, but far too fat." On the other hand, Wallace had to deplore the loss of his able lieutenant, Sir Andrew Moray of Bothwell, who, however, left a son, a younger Andrew, worthily to fill his place.

The rout of Cressingham's column had an effect upon Surrey's main body which is more difficult to understand than anything else in the whole of the war of independence. A panic seems to have smitten the English, who set fire to their end of the bridge and fled, leaving all their baggage. This is utterly unaccountable. Surrey was an experienced commander ; his troops were the best in the land and thoroughly well equipped ; Wallace's ragged levies were on the far side of the river, and the passage might easily have been defended. Anyhow, Surrey retreated as far as York, where the northern English barons were ordered to join him with fresh levies. Upon the Scottish cause this tremendous success took immediate effect. Wallace was recognised at last as the national champion ; barons and knights, as well as the common folk, trooped in to his standard, and Dundee Castle surrendered.

Wallace invades England, October, 1297. While King Edward was campaigning in France, his lieutenant, Surrey, seems to have completely lost his nerve. The Border being left undefended, Wallace entered England as far as Newcastle, which was held against him by Robert de Balliol. Robert de Brus " le viel " was still Edward's governor of Carlisle, but the king seems to have thought matters so serious that a more capable commander was required, and on 13th October Bruce was ordered to hand over the castle to the Bishop of Carlisle. Wallace ravaged Tynedale, issuing a proclamation in the name of King John Balliol, and then invested Carlisle for twenty-eight days in November and December. The Scottish commander, we may believe, possessed a very meagre pay chest; the war had to support the war, and the people of Northumberland and Cumberland suffered grievously during this winter from the depredation and exactions of the hungry Scots.

But early in the year 1298 news came that King Edward was back at Westminster and had summoned a great army to meet him at Newcastle on 6th December to avenge Surrey's misfortunes. Hemingburgh, with the customary exaggeration of clerical chroniclers, puts the numbers at 7000 horse and 80,000 foot. Needless to say that no such force has ever been put in the field in these islands. We are able to check the figures by the king's order to levy which is still in existence, and it is interesting to note the composition of a feudal army.

Northumberland	1000 foot.	Lancaster	-	3000 foot.
York -	4000 „	Cumberland	-	5000 „
Nottingham and		Westmorland	-	3000 „
Derby -	1000 „	Worcester	-	1000 „
Salop and Stafford	3000 „	North Wales	-	2000 „
Gloucester -	2000 „	Earl of Surrey's estate		
Chester -	4000 „	in Bromfield		400 „

Total, 29,400, besides men-at-arms.

Now, if it is remembered that the total population of England and Wales at this period probably did not exceed three millions, the effect of withdrawing the best manhood of certain counties from the cultivation of the soil, to follow their feudal lords in the king's service, must have had a deplorable effect upon the prosperity of the country and the welfare of the yeomen and labouring classes. I would ask you, in following the course of this warfare, to bear in mind how hardly it bore upon the commonalty of both countries. Farmers in the middle ages were as anxious to cultivate their holdings and to attend markets as they are at this day. They had to pay rent then as now, although hardly any of it was paid in silver and only part of it in kind. The most onerous part of it was the liability to military service. There was no standing army, no militia or volunteers. The baron or knight held his lands on condition of being ready to bring a fixed number of his tenants into the field whenever the government decided to go to war. One may imagine, therefore, what an amount of distress it occasioned when the summons came in the lambing season, in seed time, or in the hay or corn harvest. Everything had to be neglected, and farmers and field labourers hurried away to risk life and limb at their lord's bidding, often in a quarrel about which they knew little and cared less.

III

RISE OF BRUCE; EXECUTION OF WALLACE; DEATH OF EDWARD

A.D. 1297—1307

III

BEFORE asking you to follow the course of events any further, I would have you consider the perplexing question, in what degree was the question of national independence one in which the *communitas*—the body of the people —took a lively interest? The various races— Picts, Scots, Cumbrians, Saxons and Norsemen— who owned allegiance to Alexander III., had been too recently knit into one nation to ensure a common and homogeneous patriotism. In fact it is within our knowledge that five centuries had to pass before the Saxon Lowlander learnt to regard the Celtic Highlander without either dread or contempt—dread when he lived near the Highland border—contempt when his lot lay outside the radius of Highland raids.

Even had the natives of Scotland been of one blood and one language, there must still have existed a serious obstacle to common political sentiment and action in the difficulty of communication between different districts. How should the clansmen of Ross and Sutherland, the peasantry of Teviotdale and Clydesdale, the townspeople of Inverness and Berwick, become so simultaneously acquainted with the questions at issue as to take an intelligent and practical part in deciding them?

This is a problem which I have never seen any adequate attempt to solve, and it is with some diffidence that I venture to offer an explanation.

Scotland had been feudalised; but the majority of the feudal lords were of alien blood—Norman barons, often with interests as great in English possessions as in Scots. They could bring their tenants into the field in any cause which they chose to espouse; but that would never have inspired these tenants with that resolute, stubborn spirit of resistance which they displayed throughout the wars with England. We must look for some other agency, and I believe it is to be found among the clergy. We are not accustomed to regard bishops and other ecclesiastical dignitaries in the light of statesmen or operative politicians, but it was very different in the thirteenth century. Bishops and abbots were *ex officio* lords of parliament, and ranked higher than the lay lords or barons. A trace of this system remains in the precedence still accorded to the Archbishop of Canterbury, who ranks before any other subject after the royal family.

Prelates of the Church were not only the wealthiest but the most influential persons in the State, leaders in politics, in finance, even in war, as in the case of the famous Antony Bek, Bishop of Durham, and William de Melton, Archbishop of York. The perfect organisation of the Church of Rome kept the prelates in touch with the most remote parishes; their undisputed authority gave them complete control over the rural clergy and their people; ecclesiastical discipline, enforced under threat of excommunication in this world and everlasting torment in the next, invested the clergy with powers exceeding even those of the feudal lords.

Now circumstances had arisen which threw the whole weight of the Scottish hierarchy upon the national side. In 1218 Pope Honorius III. had confirmed the decree of Pope Alexander III. in 1174, freeing the Church of Scotland from the jurisdiction of the Church of England, and granted the clergy authority to hold Synodal Councils without the intervention of a papal legate. The president of such a council was entitled " Conservator of the Privileges of the Scottish Church." Had the English Church authorities been sagacious, they would have continued to respect those privileges until such time as Scotland had been incorporated in the English realm; but they were imprudent enough to show their hand at the outset; for, when King Edward advanced his claim as Lord Paramount of Scotland, the Archbishop of York sought to regain jurisdiction over the Scottish bishoprics. It is this, then, that we must hold accountable for the extraordinary fervour with which the Bishops of Glasgow and St. Andrews supported Bruce in his revolt against the power of England ; a revolt which, without the aid of the Church, must have proved abortive; but which, with that aid, became a truly national movement.

We left the Scots at the close of 1297 ravaging the northern English counties under William Wallace; but when King Edward came in person to Newcastle about Christmas time to take command of the great force assembled there, the Scottish leader withdrew across the Border, and on 16th February the Earl of Surrey had so far recovered from the rout of Stirling Bridge as to reoccupy Roxburgh Castle.

It was about this time, probably, that Wallace first assumed the title of Governor of Scotland for King John Balliol. While we recognise his integrity of purpose in keeping the cause of Balliol alive, the sagacity of his policy is not so clear. Balliol had abdicated and was in exile; the Scottish barons were by no means unanimous in wishing for his restoration. Some of those actually under arms with Wallace were partisans of Bruce; others again, among the most powerful barons of Scotland, were still "Edward's men." Note, for example, a letter written on

3rd July, three weeks before the disaster impending over the patriot cause, from Robert de Bruce, Earl of Carrick and future King of Scots, offering to do anything required of him in King Edward's service.[1]

In July, 1298, King Edward advanced into Scotland by way of Berwick, and encamped at Kirkliston, near Linlithgow, where his troops were put on short commons, owing to the fleet not having arrived with supplies in the Forth. The Welsh levies mutinied ; Hemingburgh says that they killed eighteen clergy and deserted in a body. The king had prepared, if he had not issued, orders for a retreat to Berwick, when his scouts brought him word that the enemy was encamped in force at Falkirk. He determined to attack them at once. On the night of 21st July, when the army was bivouacked on a moor east of Linlithgow, Edward had a narrow escape. His horse trampled on him in the darkness, and, it is said, broke two of his ribs. Nevertheless, next day Edward was in the saddle again,

[1] Bain's *Calendar*, ii. no. 995.

directing the advance. He found the Scots drawn up on rising ground near Falkirk in four circular masses of pikemen, with mounted spearmen in the centre of each mass. This is the formation so often mentioned by Barbour and Sir Thomas Gray as "the schiltrome," and very effective it often proved against mail-clad cavalry. In the intervals between the schiltromes were stationed Selkirk bowmen, the only decent archers that Scotland ever produced. They were commanded by Sir John of Bonkill, brother of James the Steward. On the flanks of the line were such cavalry as Wallace possessed, probably few in number, for they are said to have fled at the first onset. They were commanded by John Comyn of Badenoch—the Red Comyn—of whom more hereafter.

In front of the Scottish position was a peat moss. Edward having ordered his cavalry to attack, De Bigod, Earl Marshal of England, led one column round the left of the moss; Antony Bek, Bishop of Durham, led another round the right. Simultaneously they fell upon either flank of the Scots, which the flight of Comyn's cavalry had laid bare. Sir John of Bonkil fell mortally wounded ; the English chronicler, Hemingburgh, testifies to the devotion shown by his Selkirk bowmen—tall, handsome men, he calls them—who were cut down in heaps round their leader. The schiltromes stood their ground, till the English infantry came up riddling them with arrows and sling stones, which told with terrible effect on that solid formation. Macduff and Graham went down, the schiltromes wavered and broke, and a frightful slaughter began. It is idle to speculate on the number of Scots slain. Walsingham, on the English side, puts it at the preposterous figure of 60,000, probably three times the strength of Wallace's whole force. The only authentic evidence available proves that the Scots did not ply their pikes to no purpose. Edward's Exchequer Rolls record payment for 111 horses killed at Falkirk belonging to knights and esquires, not of the king's household.

The Scottish chroniclers throw the blame for

this defeat on the Red Comyn, whom they accuse of treachery in deserting the field with his squadrons. There is not the slightest ground for this charge. By the time Fordun, Bower and Wintoun were writing, Bruce was on the throne and the Comyns were in deep disgrace—an easy mark for any slander. The excellence and number of the English cavalry, supported by their famous archers, supply sufficient cause for the destruction of the weaker army.

Similar distrust is due to Hemingburgh's statement, endorsed though it be by Hailes, that the Earl of Carrick joined Wallace as soon as Edward entered Scotland. It was the aim of both English and Scottish chroniclers, from opposite motives, to make it appear that Bruce attached himself thus early to the national cause. All we know for certain is that he was receiving orders from King Edward at this time, and that he was not present at the battle of Falkirk.

The war went on in desultory fashion throughout the rest of the year. *Delirant*

reges, plectuntur Achivi. Of the misery entailed
upon all ranks of the people, let the following
incident bear witness. Wallace was waging war
in the name of John Balliol, who, as Lord of
Buittle, and son of the illustrious Devorguila,
had a strong body of adherents in Galloway.
King Edward, in order to secure the tran-
quillity of that province, caused eleven hostages
to be taken from it in October, 1297. Now
hostages, being persons of some position, were
entitled by the rules of war and diplomacy to
considerate treatment, not as prisoners, but
rather as official guests. In violation of this
honourable custom, the Earl of Surrey caused
these gentlemen to be locked into the noisome
dungeons of Lochmaben Castle. On 8th September, 1300, one of them, Robert M'Master,
was liberated, sole survivor of the horrors of
those three years.

The disaster of Falkirk was fatal to Wallace's
ascendancy with his fellow-countrymen. Early
in 1299 he went to the continent to re-enlist
the sympathies of French Philip, and to try
and induce the Pope to sanctify the Scottish

cause. Wallace being well off the scene, the Earl of Carrick appears prominent among the patriots. His master, King Edward, was in difficulties, having had to return to London to settle serious disputes with his barons. No sooner had he patched up that quarrel than the Pope's legates arrived on 3rd July, bringing the award on the dispute between England and France; peace to be secured by the marriage of King Edward to Margaret, sister of King Philip. It seemed to Bruce that Edward had too many irons in the fire to let him attend very closely to Scottish affairs: the Balliol sun had set for ever: what was there to discourage Bruce in advancing his own claim to the Scottish throne? Accordingly we find him at a meeting held in Selkirk Forest about the middle of August, among others present being the Earls of Buchan and Menteith, the Red Comyn, Lamberton, Bishop of St. Andrews, and James the Steward. They fell out among themselves: dirks flashed out and the Red Comyn had Bruce by the throat while the other Comyn—the Earl of Buchan—tackled the Bishop. However, no blood was shed; some kind of agreement was come to; before they separated, the absent Wallace was deposed from the guardianship, and Bruce, the Red Comyn and the Bishop were appointed guardians in his place. Bruce started the same day to raise Galloway and Annandale; the Comyns went off to the Highlands to assemble their forces; James the Steward and the Earl of Menteith took Clydesdale in hand. The Bishop remained at Stobo, in Selkirk Forest, and Sir Ingram de Umfraville, afterwards one of Edward's best commanders, was appointed Sheriff of Roxburgh, a post not to be confounded with the legal office known in our day. The sheriff was *vicecomes*—corresponding to a modern lord-lieutenant, but with far more extensive powers, charged with plenary administration of justice, besides being responsible for the military forces of the shire.

All these proceedings were duly reported to King Edward through a spy employed by Sir Robert Hastang, who was Edward's Sheriff of Roxburgh.

ARREST OF WALLACE

It was not through indolence that King Edward neglected the news of a fresh rising in Scotland. He was preparing for his marriage with the French princess, and in those days royal marriages were of extreme political importance. This one was planned to divorce France from the Scottish alliance, a result calculated to reduce Scotland to subjection quicker than anything else.

The marriage took place on 10th September, 1299, and at first it promised to fulfil all that was expected of it, for King Philip seized Wallace, imprisoned him and wrote offering to hand him over to King Edward. The offer, of course, was eagerly accepted ; but for some unknown reason Philip changed his mind. He not only set Wallace free, but he wrote to the Pope commending him to his favour. The result was that the Pope wrote to Edward commanding him to desist from molesting Scotland, which was a free kingdom, owning allegiance only to Holy Church. This letter was delivered to King Edward shortly after he had finished the successful siege of Caerlaverock in July,

King Philip of France arrests Wallace, 1299.

1300, the border stronghold of Sir John Maxwell. It cannot have been agreeable reading for the proud king, but even the most puissant prince had need to think twice before incurring the displeasure of the Vicegerent of God. The spiritual powers of the Pontiff were more terrible than the hosts of any monarch, for, as a devout Catholic, Edward could not doubt the dire result of excommunication upon his prospects after death. So on 30th October, at the instance of King Philip of France, he signed a truce for six months at Dumfries, and released his prisoner, Bishop Wishart of Glasgow, who swore fealty to him for the fourth time on the consecrated host, the gospels, the cross of St. Neot and the Black Rood of Scotland.

In parliament at Lincoln the Pope's letter was discussed. Nothing could have been better calculated to rally the disaffected English barons to their king. A spirited reply was drawn up. In matters spiritual, England, her king, nobles and commons were dutiful servants of Holy Church ; but in temporal affairs—"Hands off!" The answer went back to Rome with the seals appended of a hundred English earls, barons and knights.

King Edward had no intention of desisting from the conquest of Scotland. Wallace, we may believe, notwithstanding his successful diplomacy at Rome, had lost influence after his defeat at Falkirk; we hear of him no more in the field, and, when the truce expired at Pentecost, 1301, the king and the Prince of Wales conducted a campaign in the Scottish lowlands meeting with little opposition and capturing the strong castle of Bothwell.

All this time Robert Bruce, Earl of Carrick, was acting with a duplicity extraordinary even in those times of divided allegiance. As one of the Guardians of Scotland in the name of King John Balliol, perhaps we may recognise his influence in a letter addressed by the three guardians to King Edward on 13th November, 1299. They were then besieging Stirling Castle, and offered to desist from hostilities on the mediation of King Philip of France. King Edward paid no attention to this letter, and Stirling surrendered to the Scots. In April,

Robert Bruce's double-dealing, 1299–1306.

1302, Bruce and his tenants in Carrick were received to King Edward's peace—that is, owned him as their rightful king; but at that very time Bruce and his colleague, John Comyn, were negotiating with the French king, who wrote that "he fully understood the letters brought to him by Sir John Wishart and the Abbot of Jedburgh: that he was moved to the very marrow by the evils brought upon their country and that he was carefully devising how to assist them. Having in mind the dangers of the road, he would not entrust his plans to writing, but he had charged the Bishop of St. Andrews (Lamberton) to explain them to his colleagues in the guardianship."

This letter is still preserved in London, having probably come into King Edward's hands when Bishop Lamberton had thrown off the mask and was taken prisoner in July, 1306. Bruce and Lamberton were now fully committed to what would have been a perfectly legitimate enterprise, but for the repeated vows of allegiance they had made to Edward. It is with shame that we must own that the future King of Scots was at this time a treacherous conspirator. Six months after he had received King Philip's letter he attended the English parliament. You see he had to be careful about his own interests at this time, for his father, the old Lord of Annandale, was approaching his end, and his son was heir to valuable estates in England. Ostensibly, therefore, he abandoned the cause of independence, deserting Comyn and Lamberton in the guardianship, and becoming King Edward's Sheriff of Lanarkshire and Governor of Ayr Castle. He was summoned to join King Edward's army at Roxburgh for the summer campaign of 1303, with all the men-at-arms he could muster and 1000 foot from Carrick and Galloway.

On 9th February, 1304, the guardian Comyn surrendered at Strathord, receiving liberal terms for himself and his friends, on condition that they should regain the king's favour by exerting themselves to capture Wallace, who was beyond the pale of mercy. Unequal justice, this, by which trebly forsworn nobles and prelates escaped punishment, while Wallace, who had

Surrender of John Comyn, 9th February, 1304.

never sworn fealty to Edward, was to be hunted to the death. Once more, then, Sir John Comyn, Bishop Lamberton, James the Steward and other "patriots" were admitted to King Edward's presence, and there renewed their broken oaths of fealty; while on 3rd March Edward wrote to his loyal and faithful Robert de Brus, Earl of Carrick, applauding him for diligence in crushing the rebellion.

Bruce and the Bishop of Glasgow attended Edward's parliament at St. Andrews in Lent, 1304, after which Bruce hurried off to London and Essex to look after his succession and to collect his rents, for his old father was dead at last. On 13th April the king wrote to thank him for his industry in forwarding engines for the siege of Stirling; on 11th June Bruce entered into a secret bond with Bishop Lamberton, pledging them "in view of future dangers" to assist each other "against all men." That is, Lamberton was to give Bruce the powerful aid of the church in his designs upon the crown, and Bruce was to further Lamberton's purpose of establishing the inde-

Secret bond between Bruce and Lamberton, 11th June, 1304.

pendence of the Church of Scotland from English interference.

It is not agreeable to read that, three days after this bond was signed, Bruce for the fourth time solemnly swore fealty to King Edward on being served heir to his father's English estates, and that the king remitted certain debts due to him by Bruce.

Bruce, as we have seen, gave King Edward active assistance in the siege of Stirling Castle, and that siege deserves more than passing notice, both on account of the gallantry of the defenders and because it was the last appearance of King Edward in Scotland.

The garrison was commanded by Sir William de Oliphant, who, from his precipitous rock, watched the vast preparations for the siege. King Edward had written to the Prince of Wales, directing him to strip the lead from all the churches near Perth and Dunblane, to provide ammunition for thirteen great engines, the very latest inventions of military science. An oriel window was built in the king's house in the town, whence the queen and her ladies

Siege of Stirling Castle, May-July, 1304.

might watch the progress of the siege, which began about 1st May. Outside, in the town, it was a pleasant picnic in summer weather, but within the fortress provisions soon began to run short. On 20th July, the garrison being on the point of starvation, Oliphant surrendered, but King Edward would not allow any of his troops to enter the castle till he had tried the effect of a shot from a brand new engine—the *Loup-de-guerre* or war-wolf; the like of which had never been seen. The garrison were warned to seek shelter till the shot was fired, after which Oliphant and his officers were taken before the queen and then sent off to prison in England. One of these prisoners, Rafe of Haliburton, was released upon undertaking to secure Wallace. Popular tradition has whelmed in infamy the memory of Sir John Menteith as the betrayer of Wallace, but probably his part in handing him over to justice was purely official. He was King Edward's Sheriff of Dunbarton-shire and Governor of Dunbarton Castle. According to a paper in the Arundel collection Wallace was arrested in the house of one Rafe

Raye or Roy in Glasgow, whom it is reasonable to identify with Rafe of Haliburton. He would be taken before Menteith as sheriff of the county, who had no choice but to do his duty to his employer by handing the prisoner over to justice. Popular odium has attached itself to Menteith's name, just as at a later day, it attached itself to the name of Castlereagh, whose duty it became, as leader of the House of Commons, to take charge of the Six Acts, although not he, but Lord Sidmouth as Home Secretary, was primarily responsible for their provisions.

Wallace was taken to London, arriving there on 22nd August, 1305. Next day he was put upon his trial in Westminster Hall. Being arraigned as a traitor, he protested that he was no traitor to King Edward, for he had never sworn fealty to him. Nevertheless he was summarily convicted of treason, sacrilege, homicide, robbery and arson, and, on the same day, he was hanged as a homicide and robber; he was beheaded as an outlaw; for "his enormous villainy done to God and Holy

Execution of Wallace, 22nd August, 1305.

Church in burning churches and vessels containing the body of Christ and the relics of the saints," his entrails were taken out and burnt ; and as a traitor his head was set upon London Bridge, his quarters exposed at Newcastle, Berwick, Stirling and Perth.

Was Bruce a party to these proceedings ? We cannot doubt, alas, that he was consenting to the doom of Wallace, for he and Bishop Lamberton attended parliament at Westminster three weeks later, when a fresh arrangement was made for the governance of Scotland, the king appointing his nephew, John of Brittany, his lieutenant. The subjugation of Scotland was now complete, and King Edward determined to rule it wisely and leniently. Certain barons, lately in arms against him, had their lands restored to them ; orders were issued that Scottish travellers through England were to be treated as courteously as the king's English lieges ; bygones were to be bygones ; the two kingdoms were to become one in sentiment as it was now decreed they were to be one in law. King Edward had honourably attempted to effect the union by marrying the Prince of Wales to the Queen of Scotland : when that project failed, he had resort to conquest. The constitution which he bestowed upon the conquered country was as liberal in every respect as that of England, and the trust he reposed in the natural leaders of the Scottish people was touching in its completeness ; but it met with a sorry response, owing, I believe, to the adverse influence of Scottish ecclesiastics. For, of course, in the amalgamation of the two realms, the Scottish Church was to become part and parcel of the Church of England.

Once again at this parliament Bruce and Bishop Lamberton had sworn a new and more elaborate oath of allegiance on the Lord's Body, the Holy Relics and the Four Evangels. Having done so, they set out for the north to take the parts assigned to them in the new constitution of Scotland. John of Brittany could not take up his lieutenancy until after Easter, so on 16th February, 1306, King Edward appointed four custodians to conduct the government until John's arrival. One of these custodians was Bishop Lamberton, who had already broken his oath of allegiance four times.

Murder of the Red Comyn, 10th February, 1306.

Hardly was the ink on Bruce's commission dry when terrible news from the north reached King Edward in his hunting box near Winchester. Bruce had slain the Red Comyn with his own hand at Dumfries. I will not trouble you by rehearsing the various and conflicting accounts of this tragedy given by fourteenth century writers with strongly prejudiced views on one side or the other. This only must you bear in mind, if you really wish to get near the truth, that the earliest Scottish accounts were written fifty years after the event, when the dynasty of Bruce was established and it had become the interest of Scottish writers to make out the best case for King Robert.

A careful collation of the different chronicles tends to the conclusion that a secret compact existed between Robert Bruce and the Red Comyn, who, it will be remembered, had been colleagues with Bishop Lamberton in the guardianship of Scotland in 1299. When John

MURDER OF RED COMYN

Balliol abdicated in 1296, Black John Comyn the competitor became nearest heir of line under King Edward's award, and Red John Comyn had inherited his father's rights. But Bruce had inherited the rights of another competitor, and was in secret alliance with Bishop Lamberton to press them. It is alleged that he offered to make over all his lands in Scotland to Comyn, if Comyn would support him in seizing the crown, and that Comyn consented, but privily informed King Edward of the whole matter. Against that there must be set this piece of evidence that King Edward's faith in Bruce was unshaken, namely, that on 8th February, 1306, only two days before the murder, the king directed that the scutage due by Bruce on succeeding to the English estates, should be remitted.

The only certain part of the story is that Bruce and Comyn met, probably by appointment for conference, in the cloisters of the church of the Grey Friars in Dumfries; that they disagreed, high words passed, daggers flashed out, and blows were struck. Comyn, being wounded, took refuge in the church, whither Kirkpatrick of Closeburn followed and gave him the *coup-de-grace*. Sir Robert Comyn, John's uncle, was killed at the same time and place. The most favourable view that can be taken for Bruce's part in this transaction is that the deed was unpremeditated. I incline to think that Comyn showed himself unwilling to support Bruce in revolt against King Edward —perhaps threatened to denounce him as a traitor. At Peebles in 1299, when Bruce and Comyn disagreed, Comyn drew his dagger and took Bruce by the throat. Bruce, after this warning, could not give Comyn the first chance. The fatal blow was struck in a moment—the blow that was to affect the destiny of two nations for centuries to come.

The news took just a fortnight to reach King Edward at Winchester. We may surely feel some sympathy for the aged monarch, Scots though we be. The men he had trusted and honoured had accepted the favours he heaped on them and then betrayed their trust. Earnestly desiring peace in his old age, Edward was now committed to another war. He appointed Aymer de Valence, Earl of Pembroke, Governor of Scotland and commander-in-chief of the army to be assembled. In scores of letters written at this time the fiery spirit of the warrior king breathes as fiercely as ever.

As for Bruce, the die had been finally cast. He had done with his old master for ever, and, fresh from the murder of his rival, cast himself into the arms of the Church. After a hasty visit to his castle of Lochmaben, he rode to Glasgow, where Bishop Wishart received him with enthusiasm. On six separate occasions this good prelate had solemnly sworn fealty to Edward ; Bruce had done so five times ; nevertheless, so lightly did even ecclesiastics regard blasphemous perjury, he not only pronounced absolution upon Bruce from blood guilt, but he set tailors to work upon a set of coronation robes, and sent them to Scone where Bruce was crowned King of Scots on 29th March. It was the hereditary privilege of the Earls of Fife to place the crown upon a new sovereign's head ; but Duncan Macduff, the earl of that day, was

Coronation of Robert de Brus, 29th March, 1306.

faithful to his English allegiance, so his sister, Isabella, Countess of Buchan, claimed the right to do so in his place, although her husband was head of the Comyns, a near kinsman of the murdered John.

In riding from Annandale to Glasgow Bruce met a young esquire who, more than any other, was to contribute to his ultimate success. Sir William Douglas le Hardi died a prisoner in the Tower of London about 1298, his eldest son, James, being at school in Paris. The lad returned to Scotland to find his inheritance forfeited to King Edward, so he took service as page to Bishop Lamberton. When he heard of Bruce's rising, he besought his master to allow him to join him whom he believed to be rightful King of Scots. Lamberton willingly gave his consent : he gave more ; he gave young Douglas his own palfrey to carry him on a mission which he so highly approved ; and Douglas happened to meet Bruce's party on the hills near Moffat. He was to be much heard of later as the Good Sir James of Douglas, and there is no stain of perjury on his name ; for, alone among Bruce's

Good Sir James of Douglas, 1286 (?)– 1330.

officers, he never swore fealty to any king but Robert I.

At first the enterprise of the new King of Scots seemed doomed to speedy collapse. The dread sentence of the greater excommunication was passed upon him in St. Paul's Cathedral, London ; a doom which all good Catholics feared worse than death. Next, King Robert's slender force was surprised and scattered at Methven, near Perth, by Aymer de Valence, Robert himself escaping with a few of his knights into the Highland hills, where they wandered for months, suffering much privation. King Robert's brother, Niel, was captured and executed at Berwick ; his queen, his daughter, and two sisters were taken at Kildrummie, and, by King Edward's express orders, were confined in separate cages.

King Robert defeated at Methven, 26th June, 1306.

You are not to suppose, as many have done, and heaped obloquy upon King Edward for his barbarity, that these cages were like those into which the Sultan of Morocco thrusts criminals, exposed to all weathers and the view of all men. Minute directions for their construction have been preserved, showing that they were made of wooden and iron lattice, *inside* turrets of Roxburgh and Berwick Castles and the Tower of London, furnished comfortably like an ordinary apartment. The Countess of Buchan, who was also put in a cage, was allowed two waiting-women, two valets and a page, "sober and not riotous, to make her bed, and for other things necessary for the comfort of her chamber."

Many good knights taken at Methven were executed as traitors without a trial; among them Sir Simon Fraser and the Earl of Athol, who was King Edward's cousin. Sir Christopher Seton was hanged at Dumfries, his brother Sir Alexander at Newcastle, together with fifteen others. Old King Edward, though burning to take the field against "King Hobbe," as he termed the King of Scots in derision, was racked with dysentery and detained in the south; occupied in signing death-warrants and writing fiery letters of instruction to his commanders. If you would follow the King of Scots during this period of adversity, I commend you to the enchanting narrative of Archdeacon Barbour of Aberdeen, the contemporary of Chaucer, who, in his poem of "the Brus," has given a lively and faithful picture of the times. We lose sight of the king and his companions in September, when they are said to have betaken themselves to hiding in Rathlin Island, off the coast of Antrim. In February they crossed over to Arran, whence the king could survey his own earldom of Carrick, with his birthplace, Turnberry Castle, in the forefront thereof. He sent one Cuthbert to find out how matters stood on the mainland among his own tenants in Carrick, with instructions, should things seem favourable, to light a beacon on the shore. Cuthbert found things as bad as might be. Sir Henry Percy, Sheriff of Ayrshire, lay in Bruce's house of Turnberry, with 300 men billetted in the village; the whole country swarmed with English troops, and, worst of all, the people of Carrick seemed some of them indifferent, others ill disposed, to the cause of Bruce. So Cuthbert kindled no beacon.

But it was March, when farmers burn the heather, and a chance blaze near Turnberry deceived King Robert, who immediately ordered his galleys to put to sea, and landed on the Ayrshire coast before daybreak with his following of two or three hundred. Cuthbert was there to warn them of danger, for he, too, had seen the misleading blaze: but Edward Bruce, the king's brother, vowed he had had enough seafaring, and would now try his luck on land. Three hundred hungry desperadoes needed little persuasion to adventure: their plight could hardly become worse than it was. It was still dark, and all was silent in the castle and hamlet. Bruce led his men along the causeway he knew so well. Not a scabbard rattled, and the Highlanders in their deerskin brogues moved as noiselessly as so many wild cats. Food they must have at all hazards, and they sought it in the hamlet. The English soldiers were cut down as they awoke. Percy, within the keep, heard the din of slaying, yet dared not come out in the dark, not knowing what might be the strength of the enemy. Then the king's party, collecting what spoil and arms they found, made off into the hill country about Dalmellington.

Simultaneously with this exploit, the king's two brothers, Thomas and Alexander, landed from Ireland in Loch Ryan with some hundreds of Irish kernes. They fared miserably, for Sir Dougal Macdouall,[1] who was chief in those parts, attacked and cut the party in pieces, sending the Bruce brothers to King Edward at Carlisle, where they were instantly hanged.

And now we come to the most extraordinary period in the adventures of the King of Scots: would that I had time to dwell on them, but here again I must refer you to the faithful

King Robert in Glen Trool, March-May, 1307.

---

[1] The descendants of this chieftain still own extensive lands in Galloway which have been in possession of the family from a period anterior to any written record. The family divided into three branches, the head of each claiming to be chief of the clan. Each of them carries the ancient arms of the lordship of Galloway—a silver lion, crowned with gold, on an azure field. M'Douall of Logan bears the lion with the crown on its head; Macdowall of Garthland's lion is "gorged" with the crown, that is, carries it round its neck; while M'Douall of Trench (now merged in the line of Stuart, Marquess of Bute) displays his lion both crowned and gorged.

Barbour. It is worth the pains to overcome the difficulty of his antique language in order to enjoy a thoroughly romantic narrative. It is not only romantic, but trustworthy, for many of his most minute statements have been corroborated in recent years by comparison with the official papers of the English forces.

While King Robert lay ensconced with his band of ragamuffins in the recesses of Glen Trool his foes gathered closely round him, guarding every mountain pass. Twice a flying column was sent into the glen to hunt the king out, each time with the same result—sanguinary defeat of the English. Assassins were hired, if we may believe Barbour, and perished by the hand of their intended victim.

We have no information how Bruce escaped through the chain of troops posted round his hiding-place under King Edward's most renowned knights—Clifford, Vaus, de Valence, John of Lorn and Macdouall—but in the middle of May he was at Galston in Ayrshire with about 600 fighting men and as many "rangale" or rabble, as Barbour calls them.

LOUDON HILL

Choosing a good position on Loudon Hill, Battle of Loudon Hill, May, 1307. with a peat moss on each flank and a triple entrenchment along his front, he formally challenged de Valence to battle.

It seemed a hair-brained act to pit his gillie-lightfoots against the flower of English chivalry under so renowned a commander as de Valence, and it is difficult to understand how it succeeded; but the fact remained that the English were repeatedly repulsed and before nightfall were in full retreat to Ayr, leaving the King of Scots in possession of the field.

Loudon Hill proved the turning-point in Bruce's fortunes, and was followed three days later by a successful action against Sir Rafe de Monthermer, who was also driven for shelter to Ayr Castle.

These victories, small as they were in scale proved of immense importance. Barons and knights, whose sympathies went with Bruce, but who had held aloof from what appeared to be a hopeless cause, now joined the national flag, besides which there were plenty of broken men and outlaws who flocked in as recruits. Still, had King Edward lived and remained on good terms with France, it is hardly possible that he would have been baffled in reducing the Scots to subjection, supported as he was by the powerful Earls of Buchan, Fife, March and others, besides chieftains of the ancient race like Lorn and Macdouall of Galloway. Sheer weight of numbers and superiority of resources, in the strong hands of Edward Longshanks, must have prevailed in the end, even against one so redoubtable as his former vassal.

Death of Edward I., 7th June, 1307.

But the days of the Hammer of the Scots, as Edward's courtiers named him, were numbered. He was so far recovered as to leave Carlisle, intending to take command of the forces in Scotland; but he had not ridden far when his dysentery returned and he breathed his last on 7th June, 1307, at Burgh-on-Sands, within sight of the land that had so stubbornly defied his authority.

It is difficult to persuade Scotsmen to discard prejudice in their judgment of Edward the First. They cannot forgive him for the execution of Wallace; but if I have been successful in unravelling the motives which regulated Edward's dealings with Scotland, in tracing from his first design of peaceable union of the crowns by marriage the various phases by which he was forced by the internal feuds of parties in Scotland to the conclusion that union could only come through conquest, then it is hard to resist the conclusion that, after that conquest had been effected, and King Edward's authority established in the land, those who resisted it took their lives in their hands—in short, technically had to be regarded as rebels.

That, at all events, is the case for the English king. And, if the execution of Wallace was a judicial murder, are the Scottish leaders clear of a share in it? Bruce, Comyn, Bishop Lamberton—they were all in high favour with King Edward at the time, yet none of them raised a finger in intercession for their former comrade-in-arms. I am afraid that the deeper the reproach that is heaped upon Edward's memory for the doom of Wallace, the greater share of shame falls to Robert Bruce who profited by what Wallace had accomplished without his help. I think that, if we have in mind the great change that has taken place in the standard of humanity since the fourteenth century, we can afford to acknowledge that, if the cause of national independence had a splendid champion in Robert the Bruce, it had a noble enemy in the greatest of the Plantagenets.

IV

THE TURN OF THE TIDE

A.D. 1307—1322

IV

NOTHING could have been more propitious to the cause of Bruce and of Scottish independence than the death of Edward I. His son, Edward of Carnarvon, inherited neither his father's resolute spirit nor his aptitude for war. The first act of the new king was to create Piers de Gaveston Earl of Cornwall, a man whom Edward I. had always held in abhorrence, and with whom he had forbidden the Prince of Wales to hold any intercourse. Gaveston, a showy and insolent Gascon, became prime favourite with Edward II., and immediately began that series of insults to those who had enjoyed the late king's confidence, for which ultimately he paid with his head. Especially did he love to affront Aymer de Valence, whom he sneered at as a Jew, because of his dark complexion.

King Edward, advised by Gaveston, led the army, which his father had collected at Carlisle, as far as Cumnock in Nithsdale, whence they received orders to retire on 25th August without striking a blow. Gaveston and his master considered that both of them had been long enough separated from the ease and pleasure of life in the southern capital.

All through this summer Bruce had lurked in the fastnesses of the Galloway hills. These southern uplands are hallowed in the remembrance of our people chiefly through the sufferings of the Covenanters ; but that should not obliterate their earlier glory as the scene of Bruce's adventures—the true birthplace and cradle of Scottish independence. From this secure retreat Bruce vigilantly watched the movements of his enemy, too wise to risk any encounter in the open after his success at Loudon Hill, but quick to take the offensive the moment the English army began to retire.

Early in the autumn of 1307 he moved to the north, leaving Sir James Douglas to raise and organise forces in the south. Douglas began by capturing his own castle of Douglas. It was the morning of Lanark fair, in the autumn of 1307. Douglas planted a strong ambush near the castle, and made fourteen of his men to pull countrymen's frocks over their armour, and so lead horses past the castle carrying sacks stuffed with grass. Douglas knew that the garrison, being short of provender, were not likely to allow what looked like a train of provision to pass unmolested, and, sure enough, out sallied the constable, Sir John de Wanton, at the head of an armed party. Before he could overtake the supposed rustics, they had thrown off their frocks, flung the sacks to the ground, leapt into the saddles, and there was Sir John face to face with a little troop of well-armed cavalry. Douglas came out of his ambush, and the English, taken front and rear, were nearly all killed and the castle surrendered. Sir John de Wanton was among the slain, and, according to Barbour, there was found upon his body a letter from his lady-love, consenting to marry him only on condition that he should

Recapture of Douglas Castle, September, 1307.

prove himself "ane gud bacheler" by keeping
for a whole year

> "The aventurous castell of Douglass,
> That to kep sa peralous was."

Barbour's spirited poem is full of stirring
episode and chivalrous exploit, and great is
the temptation to dwell upon his record; but
if we are to keep abreast of the main current,
it is only here and there that I can bring some
of these deeds to your notice.

Notwithstanding his early successes and the
growing dissensions of the English, the King
of Scots found little encouragement at first in
the north. Barbour puts the armed force with
him at no more than 700, and it is surprising
that the Earl of Buchan failed to capture him
while he lay sick at Inverurie. So badly had
King Robert's health suffered from long ex-
posure and privation that he had to be moved
from place to place in a litter. By the middle
of May, 1308, he was in the saddle again, with
enough troops to defeat Buchan at Old Meldrum
and to waste his lands in a destructive raid long
remembered as "the Herschip of Buchan."

The Her-
schip of
Buchan,
May, 1308.

From this time forward the cause of the King of Scots kept the ascendant. King Edward had troubles enough at home to cause him to wish the Scottish quarrel off his hands. The clouds were gathering thickly round him. The barons were furiously jealous of his Gascon favourite, Piers Gaveston, and refused to allow Edward to be crowned till he agreed to allow their demands to be submitted to parliament. Edward declined to treat directly with King Robert, but he gave the Wardens of Scotland, Umfraville, Earl of Angus and Sir William de Ros of Hamelake, permission to arrange a truce until Easter, 1309. If overtures were made to King Robert, he was far too resolute to listen to them. Every day brought him fresh adherents, among them being several knights who had done good service to Edward I., but were disgusted with the course of affairs under the new reign.

Sir James Douglas made a most important capture in Tweeddale, where Aymer de Valence's lands had been forfeited by King Edward, because his tenants had risen in support of King Robert.

Exploit on
the Water
of Lyne,
1308 or
1309.
Late one night Douglas came to a house on
the Water of Lyne, intending to rest there, but
found it already occupied.   He crept under the
window, and, listening, recognised the speech of
Englishmen.   He set his men round the house
and, by a sudden assault, overpowered those
within.   Among them were two prisoners of
immense importance, namely, King Robert's
nephew, Thomas Randolph, and Sir Alexander,
brother of James the Steward and first cousin
of Douglas himself.   Randolph, according to
Barbour, had been in King Edward's service at
Cumnock, when King Robert was beset in Glen
Trool.   He was now barely of age, and when he
was brought before King Robert, he defied his
uncle, taunting him with cowardice because he
avoided open encounter with the English and
had recourse to treacherous ambuscades.   King
Robert clapped the lad in prison, where a few
weeks of reflection brought him to a more dutifu
frame of mind.   He transferred his allegiance
to Robert, was created Earl of Moray, and
became the chivalrous rival of Sir James Douglas
in devotion to the cause of independence.

GALLOWAY SUBDUED

In the course of 1309, Edward Bruce, the king's brother, wrested Galloway from Sir Ingelram de Umfraville, formerly a champion of Balliol's independence, but now, as a near kinsman of the murdered Comyn, an inveterate foe of King Robert. About the same time King Robert entered Argyll in person and subdued it, John of Lorn escaping in his galleys to England.

King Edward succeeded better in diplomacy than he did in the field. In this year he won over Pope Clement V., and persuaded him to excommunicate King Robert for " damnably persevering in iniquity." Nevertheless, so great was the disorder in Edward's own realm, and so staunch was the King of France in support of the Scots, that in August, 1309, Edward was forced to negotiate for a truce. If he succeeded, the truce must have been a short one, for in September he invaded Scotland in great force. King Robert's policy was to avoid encounter and to fall back before his enemy, leaving the country bare of cattle and provender, so that when spies reported to King Edward that the

Scots were encamped on a moor near Stirling, the English were unable to continue the pursuit for want of supplies, and went into winter quarters at Berwick.

There King Edward seems to have remained until the spring of 1311, when he went to London reluctantly enough to meet the parliament he had so long delayed to summon, and, when it met, he found his barons far more eager for the downfall of the detested Piers Gaveston than for the discomfiture of the King of Scots.

King Robert raids Northumberland, 1311–1312.

No sooner had King Edward quitted the border than his vigilant foe assumed the offensive. In August, 1311, and February, 1312, King Robert raided Northumberland and Cumberland, refraining, says the English chronicler of Lanercost, from killing men or burning houses, but exacting heavy contributions in money—£2000 from the county of Northumberland alone. A like sum was exacted from each of the four northern counties by Edward Bruce after midsummer as the price of a truce of two years.

One after another the English garrisons, ill-supported, or not supported at all, by their own government, capitulated or were overcome by parties of Scots, and the fortifications in every case were razed or dismantled by King Robert's special command. Forfar fell some time in 1312; Perth, a far stronger place, was taken by assault in January, 1313; Dumfries followed in February. It was commanded by Sir Dougal Macdouall of Galloway, who had delivered King Robert's two brothers to the Carlisle gallows in 1307. Robert spared his life; but perhaps we should not attribute this entirely to magnanimity, seeing how rich a ransom the custom of war entitled the victor to exact from a prisoner of Macdouall's wealth and import-ance. There was another, and more creditable, reason why King Robert never executed English prisoners taken in war against him. King Edward did so frequently, as I have explained in former lectures—seventeen knights hanged in one day at Newcastle. But these, and scores of others, were tried and condemned by the law of the land as rebels and traitors, having broken their oaths of allegiance to the English king. Macdouall, and the many other prisoners taken by King Robert, had never sworn allegiance to him. He himself, having seized the throne, had no title to treat them as rebels, and, had he caused them to be executed, he would have been guilty of murder. We know, besides, from other circumstances that his disposition was the reverse of sanguinary. In several cases he released English knights taken in war without even holding them to ransom, which was a very unusual kind of forbearance in those days.

Continued success of the King of Scots, 1313–1314.

To resume, then, the series of Scottish successes, Linlithgow Castle was captured by stratagem in the autumn of 1313, through the gallantry of a simple peasant named Bunnock. Sir Richard Livingstone held it for King Edward with a mixed garrison of English, Scots, and Irish, who had been employed in cutting hay during the summer in the meadows beside the loch. Bunnock, having got himself hired to cart the hay into the castle, placed a party in ambush near at hand at a time when the garrison were busy at the corn harvest. He

concealed eight armed men in his wagon under
the hay, and gave the lad who led the horses
a sharp axe, with instructions how to use it.
Then he brought his load to the castle gate;
the porter threw all wide to admit him; but
Bunnock turned the horses so that the wagon
got jammed in the gateway. The boy slashed
the ropes of the drawbridge with his axe so that
the bridge could not be raised, the eight stout
fellows jumped out of the hay, killed the luck-
less porter, overpowered the few soldiers within
the castle, and the ambush running up made all
secure before the rest of the garrison returned
from the harvest field. And thus the important
pele of Linlithgow was won for King Robert.

On Shrove Tuesday, in the following year, Sir
James Douglas, by another romantic stratagem
got possession of Roxburgh Castle, the most
important fortress on the Border, commanding
as it did Teviotdale and Upper Tweeddale, and
King Robert, according to his invariable practice,
caused it to be razed to the ground. During
the same season of Lent, young Thomas
Randolph scored his first success in his uncle's

Capture of Roxburgh Castle, February, 1314.

service by taking Edinburgh Castle, reputed impregnable, by night assault. By the spring of 1314 the only important Scottish fortresses flying the English flag were Berwick, Stirling, Bothwell and possibly Lochmaben.

The most devout Scottish patriot cannot but feel some pity for the English commanders and their troops, left without any support or encouragement from their own king, in presence of an enemy growing daily in strength and activity. Garrison after garrison had to yield to force of numbers or stress of starvation. A crowning disaster was drawing near—a dire humiliation for the proud chivalry of England.

Edward Bruce had closely invested Stirling Castle from Lent till Midsummer, 1313. Then he consented to suspend hostilities on Sir Philip Mowbray, the governor, agreeing to surrender if he was not relieved before Midsummer Day, 1314. King Robert was mightily displeased when he heard of this treaty. Mowbray's cry for succour was the very thing wanted to rally the English barons to their incompetent king, and to commit King Robert to a pitched battle, which, as we have seen, it was his deliberate strategy to avoid. However, Edward Bruce's knightly word had been pledged, and the King of Scots, often as he had broken faith in the past, was not going to shrink from helping his brother to redeem the pledge.

Piers Gaveston by this time had expiated his offences on the scaffold of Warwick, and Edward's barons blithely responded to the call to arms. The army mustered at Wark on 11th June, 1314. Its strength has been usually estimated at 100,000, but this is undoubtedly an exaggeration. The English fleet, co-operating with the army, would have plenty to do in landing supplies for 50,000 troops, which is the utmost figure that can be justified by examining the Patent Rolls, which account for 21,540 English infantry, probably 5000 or 6000 cavalry, and large contingents from Wales and Ireland. As for the strength of the Scots, which Barbour puts at 30,000, the only guide to an estimate is the general concurrence of writers that King Robert's forces were equal to about one-third of the English. But he had the great advantage of

Campaign of Bannockburn, June, 1314.

choosing the place of encounter. He took up a position facing south on undulating ground with his right flank resting on the Torwood, his left on the carse at Bannockburn. Along front of the position flowed the Bannock, an insignificant brook, almost level with its banks between Parkmill on the west and Beaton's mill on the east, a distance of less than a mile. Outside these points the banks are precipitous, wooded cliffs, impracticable for cavalry ; therefore the front of Edward's great army had to be much reduced before a crossing could be effected.

But this was very far from all. Besides the Bannock there were two bogs, now drained, skirting either side of the ancient causeway along which the enemy had to defile. These bogs lay on the north side of the Bannock, between that stream and the Scottish front. King Robert caused the ground between these two bogs and also the hard land opposite and outside his right flank to be honeycombed with pits, blinded with sods resting on small sticks, as a protection against cavalry—the arm in which the English were strong and he was very weak.

BANNOCKBURN

At sunrise on Sunday, 23rd June, mass was celebrated in the Scottish camp, albeit the king was still under ban of excommunication. The English advanced guard came in sight on the rising ground near Plean, having marched about nine miles from Falkirk. The weather was intensely hot, the troops were exhausted by the march, a council of war was held and decided to postpone the attack till next day.

There is much confusion in the accounts given by different writers of the order of events. I prefer to follow the narrative of Sir Thomas Gray, author of the *Scalacronica*, first, because he was a soldier and, unlike the monkish and therefore inexpert chroniclers who are usually relied on, he understood what he was writing about ; and, second, because he must have got his facts from his father, also Sir Thomas Gray, who was taken prisoner on the Sunday and actually watched the battle on Monday from within the Scottish camp.

When the main body of English halted at Plean on Sunday 23rd, the Earl of Gloucester pressed forward with the advanced guard, his

Affair of Randolph's Field, 23rd June, 1314.

141

young knights being eager for a brush with the enemy. The King of Scots rode up and down in front of his line of columns mounted on a palfrey. In accordance with chivalrous usage, an English knight rode forward alone to challenge a Scottish champion to single combat. Gray says it was Piers de Mountforth, but the English chronicler Trivet was probably better informed; he says it was Sir Henry de Bohun, nephew of the Earl of Hereford. As the English knight was armed at all points and riding a powerful charger, it must have been with horror that the Scots saw their king take up the challenge in person. De Bohun laid his lance in rest and charged. The king caused his pony nimbly to avoid the shock and, rising in his stirrups, smote the English champion such a blow with his axe as clove his head from crown to chin. It is easy to imagine to what a pitch of confidence and enthusiasm the Scots were roused by this exploit, enacted on that summer Sunday morning in plain view of both armies.

Meanwhile Gloucester had detached a squadron of heavy cavalry, 300 strong, under Sir Robert de Clifford, to outflank the Scottish line on the left and, keeping out of sight on the low ground, establish communications with the garrison of Stirling. This was precisely what King Robert had foreseen would be attempted, and had the movement been successful, Stirling Castle must have been reckoned as relieved, Mowbray and his garrison would have been freed from their pledge of neutrality and been able to threaten the Scots upon their rear. The king, therefore, had specially charged his nephew Thomas Randolph to guard against any such attempt, but Randolph, we may suppose, like the rest of the Scottish army, had their attention rivetted on the king's duel with Bohun. King Robert, having floored his antagonist. instantly detected the English horse moving round his left flank, and sent a sharp rebuke to Randolph, telling him he had "let fall a rose from his chaplet." Randolph, stung by the taunt, proceeded to execute a manœuvre which it would be impossible to understand without Gray's explanation of it. It has generally been

supposed that Randolph set out with cavalry
to overtake de Clifford ; he certainly could not
intercept him with infantry. But in the whole
Scottish army there were but 500 cavalry,
commanded by Sir Robert de Keith, and these
were not brought into action on Sunday. Randolph's party was on foot. When the English
knights saw them hastening along the higher
wooded ground—" Wait a little " ; cried Sir
Henry Beaumont, "let them come on : get
them out in the open."

" Sir," said Sir Thomas Gray, " I fear they
be too many for us." To which Beaumont
made the contemptuous retort—" Look you !
If you are afraid, you can ride away."

" Sir," replied stout old Sir Thomas, " it is
not from fear that I shall retire this day."

With these words he ranged up alongside of
de Beaumont and Sir William D'Eyncourt and
charged the Scots, who were in the usual formation of schiltrome, resembling one of our infantry
squares, each front rank man kneeling with the
butt of his pike firmly planted on the ground,
the rear rank men standing, armed with longer

pikes. Archery and sling stones were the only effective arms to bring against such a hedge of steel, and Clifford's party had neither archers nor slingers with them. Charge after charge was repulsed. Sir William D'Eyncourt fell dead in the first onslaught : Sir Thomas Gray's horse was piked and his rider taken prisoner. The English, seeing Sir James Douglas bringing up a column to support Randolph, took to flight.

The scene of this conflict—the Quatre Bras of Bannockburn—was probably the ground now known as Randolph's Field, at the south end of Melville Terrace in the suburbs of Stirling. Sir Thomas Gray the younger sorrowfully remarks that the Scots had learnt how to meet cavalry on foot from the Flemings, who in that manner had discomfited the Count of Artois and all the chivalry of France at Courtraye in 1302.

After this double discomfiture Gloucester fell back upon the main body of the English. As for the Scots, the requirements of the chivalrous code had been amply fulfilled. They had kept the appointed tryst, met and defeated their enemy in open field, and their king had killed the English champion. King Robert immediately prepared to strike his camp and resort to his usual strategy of falling back and wasting the country before the enemy. But at midnight, when the Scots were on the point of evacuating the position and marching off into the wild district of the Lennox, Sir Alexander de Seton, a Scottish knight in the English service, rode to King Robert's tent in the Torwood, and assured him that, if he ever meant to be King of Scotland, now was his time, for the English, said he, were dispirited and disaffected. On hearing this, says Sir Thomas Gray, King Robert countermanded the retreat, resolved to await the enemy's attack on the morrow.

Battle of Bannockburn, 24th June, 1314.

At dawn on St. John's day, the Abbot of Inchaffray celebrated mass in the Scottish camp, and shortly after sunrise the troops moved out to the alignment chosen by the king. While they were taking up their positions, the English host came in view, making a brilliant and magnificent display in the morning sunlight. It is recorded

that when King Edward beheld the mean array
opposed to him, with none of the gorgeous
heraldry and sumptuous armour which blazed in
his own columns, he asked if that rabble really
meant to fight. Old Sir Ingelram de Umfraville,
riding in attendance, replied that assuredly they
would fight, and advised that the English
should make feint to retire, which he knew
would tempt the Scots to break their formidable
"schiltromes" and rush into a disorderly pursuit.

"See!" cried King Edward, "am I not right?
They kneel for mercy." For the Abbot of
Inchaffray was moving along the front with a
crucifix, and each division knelt as he passed.

"You speak sooth now, Sire," said Sir Ingelram; "they crave mercy, but not from you.
It is God's mercy they implore. These men
will never fly: they will win all or die."

"We shall see," said Edward, and bade the
trumpets sound "Advance!"

The English moved in nine columns or divi-
sions. In advance rode the Earl of Gloucester
with 500 men-at-arms. Owing to the boggy
ground which I have described, they could not

deploy until at the foot of the rising ground on which the Scots were posted. The English chronicler, De la More, describes them as being thrown into disarray by the pits dug on the hard ground in front of the Scottish right, but their slow advance was covered by a cloud of archers, which severely galled Edward Bruce's division. His position was critical, for the enemy was pressing his attack in front. The fortune of the day was decided by King Robert's use of his small force of cavalry, 500 lances under Sir Robert de Keith. He ordered them to clear the ground of the English archers, which thing they did effectively. Then it became an affair of heavy cavalry against foot-soldiers in schiltrome. In vain the gallant Gloucester strove to break that fence of cruel pikes. He met a soldier's death in the attempt.

Behind the cavalry, the whole weight of the English columns was pressing onward, disarrayed for want of room. They could not deploy to their right because of Halbert's Bog, protecting the Scottish centre—so Randolph moved to support Edward Bruce, and King

ROUT OF THE ENGLISH

Robert moved up his reserve to occupy the ground vacated by Randolph. The whole ground from Parkmill to Halbert's Bog, about half a mile square, was now one disordered mass of English soldiers and knights. Wounded horses plunged down among them from the mellay in front; the pressure from the columns in rear became intolerable, and now it was the turn of the Selkirk bowmen, who played on the helpless mass with murderous effect. The splendid English array was hopelessly broken. Men jammed into one mass of living, dead and dying, be they never so willing, cannot obey orders, be they never so clearly given.

It is said that at this moment an unforeseen and accidental circumstance turned the rout into a panic. The Scottish camp-followers had been watching the conflict from the security of Gillies Hill.[1] They had seen the repulse of Gloucester's cavalry, the rout of the English archers, the advance of the king's reserve, and

[1] The name commemorates the position of the Scots train of "gillies" or serving-men.

the dire confusion of the English columns. Now was the moment for plunder. They rushed down the hill with wild cries, and the English, mistaking them for a reinforcement, broke into general flight. A fearful scene of butchery followed. About a mile and a half from the field, just south of Bannockburn House, is a place still called the Bloody Fauld, where a body of English rallied for a stand. It is said that they perished to a man.

King Edward had witnessed the action from Charter's Hill, almost opposite the Scottish right. When his army took to flight, he was very nearly taken by some Scottish knights fighting on foot. They seized the trappings of his charger, but Edward, who was an immensely powerful man, felled them with his mace. His horse was killed, but a fresh one was brought up for him, and Aymer de Valence told him the day was lost and he must fly. His other attendant, Sir Giles de Argentine, said: "Sire, I was placed in charge of your rein: seek your own safety. For myself—

I am not used to flee : nor will I do so now. I commend you to God ! " Then he spurred forward into the thick of Edward de Brus's column, shouting " Argentine ! Argentine ! " and was hacked to pieces.

King Edward and his bodyguard then rode to the gate of Stirling Castle and claimed admission ; but Governor Moubray begged him to hold on his way, as the place must needs be surrendered. So he turned his horse, threaded his way through the Torwood and galloped away for Linlithgow and thence to Dunbar, where the Earl of March received him to shelter. He vowed that, if he escaped, he would dedicate a house for poor Carmelites to the Mother of God, and, having reached Berwick in a small boat on 27th June, he afterwards redeemed his pledge by building what is now Oriel College, Oxford.

The total losses of the English on that terrible Midsummer Day may never be reckoned. Twenty-one barons and bannerets were killed, including such renowned knights as the Earl of Gloucester, nephew of the king, the veteran de Clifford,[1] Sir Pagan de Typtloft and Sir Edmund de Mauley, Marshal of England. The English chronicler, Walsingham, says that besides these 700 gentlemen of coat-armour perished. Twenty-two barons and ban-nerets were taken prisoners, among them the Earls of Hereford and of Angus, besides sixty knights and many prisoners.

The common soldiers who escaped from the field fared miserably, the country people rising and killing them as they tried to reach the Border.

On the Scottish side the only knights of renown killed were Sir William de Vipont and Edward Bruce's dearest friend, Sir Walter de Ros.

You may remember that the Queen of Scots and her two daughters had been prisoners in England for eight years. On 2nd October they were released, together with the Bishop

[1] Robert, 1st Lord de Clifford, ancestor of the present Edward Southwell Russell, 26th Lord de Clifford through the female line ; and, in the male line, of Lewis Clifford, 8th Lord Clifford of Chudleigh, and of Sir George Clifford of Flaxbourne, New Zealand.

of Glasgow and the young Earl of Mar in exchange for the Earl of Hereford.

This crushing defeat, the loss of all his stores, the capture or death of many of his ablest generals, and, above all, the blow to English prestige, might have disposed King Edward to listen favourably to overtures for a lasting peace which King Robert, after wasting the northern counties of England, addressed to him in his parliament at York held in September. Negotiations were opened at Dumfries between the commissioners of both nations, but they came to nought, because of the flat refusal of the English to recognise the kingship of Robert Bruce.

King Edward was now deeply involved in fresh disputes with his own barons. During the next six years the dalesmen of the northern counties were left to their own resources to keep the Scots at bay, and most stoutly they did so under the leadership of William Melton, Archbishop of York, and those most warlike Bishops, Antony Bek of Durham and John de Halton of Carlisle.

It would be wearisome to follow in detail the long succession of raids made by the Scots upon English soil, including the unsuccessful siege of Carlisle by King Robert in person in the summer of 1315. Enriched by the ransoms of his prisoners, and by the indemnities levied upon English counties and towns, the King of Scots was tempted to make what seems to us the one blunder he committed after finally taking up the cause of Scottish independence. The O'Neills of Ulster invited him to come and deliver their country from English oppression, and offered the crown of Ireland to his brother, Edward Bruce. Before committing himself to what was to prove a disastrous enterprise, King Robert must have weighed the advantage of dividing the English forces against the imprudence of dividing his own. It would be no trifling advantage, he may have thought, to plant on the flank of England a power friendly to Scotland. Moreover, King Robert had no son ; his own health had suffered sorely during these strenuous years ; therefore, at a parliament held at

The Scots invade Ireland, 1315.

154

Ayr in April, 1315, Edward Bruce was appointed heir presumptive to the crown of Scotland. If, then, having become King of Ireland, he should succeed to the throne of Scotland also, his realm in extent and population would not be inferior to King Edward's. A seductive vision, but, as we know, it was never realised. Edward Bruce, indeed, was crowned King of Ireland on 2nd May, 1316, and King Robert joined him in the autumn, leaving his own kingdom under the governance of his son-in-law, Walter Stewart, and Sir James Douglas. But if these two kings imagined that the native Irish would rise as a nation to welcome them as deliverers from English rule, they were grievously mistaken. The Irish hated all Norman invaders equally, and the campaigns of Edward Bruce were a dismal chronicle of slaughter and rapine, starvation and disease. Edward Bruce's reign ended with his death at the battle of Dundalk in October, 1318. He had no legitimate offspring, so, at a parliament held at Scone in December, the vacant succession to the Scottish crown was settled on Robert, only son of Walter Stewart and Princess Marjorie, daughter of King Robert.

The English recover the Isle of Man, 1315.

Meanwhile not a solitary gleam of good fortune had shone upon the English arms since, in the spring of 1315, John of Lorn had recaptured the Isle of Man, which King Robert had annexed in June, 1313.

Among the numerous successes gained by the Scots on the Border, there is one so picturesque—so thoroughly in accord with the hare-brained chivalry of the period—that I will pause to mention it before passing on to more important events.

Douglas encounters the "Peacock of the North," 1316(?).

A certain knight of Northumberland, Sir Robert Neville, was known as the Peacock of the North, so gay was his attire and so debonair his manner. He declared it made him sick to hear perpetually about the prowess of the Black Douglas, and pledged his knightly word to attack him whenever and wherever he saw his banner displayed. Douglas, hearing of this, rode all night to Berwick, where Neville was in garrison, and in the morning unfurled his banner—the well-known azure field with three silver stars—on a height before the city walls. To ensure the Peacock's attention, he fired some of the neighbouring villages. Neville rode forth at once with a party of picked men-at-arms. Douglas challenged him to single combat, which the gallant English knight accepted, and paid the penalty of his life. Then the two parties of horsemen engaged, and three of Neville's brothers were among the prisoners taken. They were held to ransom for 2000 marks each.

Thomas Randolph had now been created Earl of Moray, and in March, 1318, he and Douglas captured Berwick by night escalade. At this time the Pope, John XXII., sent two cardinals to command King Robert to make a truce of two years with the King of England. At the same time he wrote to King Edward, apologising for addressing Robert Bruce as King of Scots, his only reason for doing so being that it was very important that the said Robert Bruce should receive the Papal letters, and that he contumaciously refused to receive

The Scots capture Berwick, March, 1318.

any that were not addressed to him under his royal style.

The loss of Berwick was too serious a blow to be received passively by King Edward, so, having composed for the nonce his quarrel with the Earl of Lancaster, he assembled some 12,000 troops at Newcastle in the spring of 1319, and proceeded to besiege Walter Stewart, who was in command of Berwick. He had now got the Pope on his side, who allowed him to appropriate £2000 out of the funds collected for a crusade. Instead of marching to the relief of Berwick, Douglas and Moray made a diversion in favour of the besieged by a more than usually destructive raid by Carlisle as far as the walls of York. Archbishop Melton did his best, but King Edward had taken away all the best fighting men of the district. On 20th September a motley force of clergy and laymen ventured to oppose the hardy veterans under Douglas and Moray at Myton-on-Swale, and were defeated so thoroughly that the affair was called in derision the Chapter of Myton. The archbishop's servants had

The "Chapter of Myton," 20th September, 1319.

stupidly brought his plate in the baggage train, which, with all other movables, fell a prize to the victors. King Edward had now to look after the safety of his own kingdom. The siege of Berwick was raised on 24th September.

Thirteen years had now passed since Robert de Brus, an excommunicated assassin and proclaimed rebel, had been crowned King of Scots, and then had to fly before the whole armed force of both kingdoms. Now, the whole nation owned him as king; twice had his so-called overlord been driven across the border, after bringing all the power at his command—military, diplomatic and spiritual, to bear on the subjugation of the weaker, poorer country. Beaten in the field, disheartened by the disaffection of his barons, Edward was now forced to sue for peace. King Robert granted him a truce for two years from Christmas, 1319.

The Pope, not having foreseen this total collapse of King Edward's power, had issued fresh instructions for the excommunication of King Robert a third time, unmindful, it would appear, of the fact that the more curses were heaped upon the Bruce, the brighter shone fortune upon his arms. After Edward's failure at Berwick, the excommunication was postponed and the Pope summoned "the nobleman Robert de Brus, governing the kingdom of Scotland" to appear before him at Avignon with the Scottish bishops. To this summons King Robert paid no attention, because it was not addressed to him as king. From the altars, therefore, of London, York and Carlisle was fulminated the dire sentence of excommunication from which the Pope directed that King Robert was never to be released until he was at the point of death.

But although the king returned no answer to the Pope's letter, the Scottish nation did so through their parliament at Arbroath. This memorable document is long and closely reasoned, but it contains one sentence which should never fade from the memory of Scotsmen.

"WHILE THERE EXIST A HUNDRED OF US, WE WILL NEVER SUBMIT TO ENGLAND. We fight—not for glory, wealth or honour, but for that liberty which no virtuous man shall survive."

These resolute sentiments did not fail to make an impression on Pope John. He addressed a letter to King Edward, directing him to make a lasting peace with the Scots. Edward appointed commissioners to treat with those of King Robert at Carlisle; but, unfortunately, he did not act sincerely in the matter. A peace conference imposes on both parties not only a cessation of hostilities, but a suspension of intrigue. King Edward never desisted his attempt through his agents to sap the loyalty of King Robert's subjects. The Archbishop of York did not scruple to promise release from excommunication to all deserters; but although this bait caught a few malcontent or nervous persons, the Scottish nation as a whole remained faithful to King Robert.

I must pass rapidly over the events of the next few years. After the execution of the Earl of Lancaster in 1322, Edward found himself able to make a third invasion of Scotland;

Invasion and counter-invasion, 1322.

but King Robert swept the country bare before him, and, after lying three days about Edinburgh and Leith, the English army was forced to retire whence they came, owing to want of supplies. Nevertheless, that invasion cost our nation dear, for Holyrood and Melrose Abbey were sacked, and the beautiful Monastery of Dryburgh was burnt to the ground.

Battle of Biland, October, 1322. King Robert was now strong enough to exact instant vengeance. He crossed the Solway on 1st October and marched as far as Biland in Yorkshire, levying heavy tribute from the towns in his route. Finding King Edward strongly posted on a ridge between Biland and Rievaulx, he inflicted upon him so sudden a defeat that Edward lost all his baggage and escaped with great difficulty, being pursued by Walter Stewart to the very gates of York.

King Edward was now reduced to the humiliation of suing for a truce; but he addressed himself not to the King of Scots, but to the men of Scotland. King Robert declined to negotiate on such terms, and King Edward was compelled to give him the royal title he had won, whereupon, on 30th May, 1323, a truce was proclaimed to last for thirteen years. For more than a year after this negotiations were carried on with the object of converting this truce into a permanent peace; but they came to nought, owing to the persistency with which the English delegates urged the vexed claim of overlordship and for the surrender of Berwick. The Pope refused to absolve King Robert and his subjects from sentence of excommunication until these points were conceded; but the Scots dauntlessly defied him, having long since learnt to discount the terrors of bell, book and candle.

V

FINAL DISMISSAL OF THE BALLIOLS

A.D. 1327—1364

V

KING EDWARD II. did not live to see the end of the truce he had obtained, for he was forced to abdicate on 24th January, 1327, and soon afterwards was done to shameful death. King Robert had employed the time well in developing the resources of his kingdom, and his parliament of Cambuskenneth in 1326 is memorable as the first in which the representatives of the burghs sat in council with the earls and barons. This parliament was specially important, inasmuch as Queen Elizabeth of Scotland had borne a son after twenty years of marriage, which reopened the question of the succession. Parliament, therefore, passed an Act of Settlement, recognising this Prince David as heir-apparent.

The immediate effect of the revolution in England, whereby Edward III., a youth of fifteen, came to the throne, was disastrous to the cause of international peace. It is true that one of Edward's earliest acts was to confirm the truce and to appoint commissioners to negotiate for a durable peace; but each nation was nervously jealous of the other; any movement of troops on either side of the Border aroused suspicion; finally King Robert, having failed to obtain redress against certain English pirates, sent openly to the English king renouncing the truce.

Campaign of Weardale, 1327. Once more the bale fires flared from height to height along the Border; once more the Border farmers were summoned from peaceful toil to reap a bloodier harvest than they had sown, and to march under those tried comrades in arms, Douglas and Moray, the right and left arms of the Scottish monarchy. They entered England on 15th June, 1327, and there followed the memorable campaign of Weardale —memorable, because therein the young Edward received his baptism of fire, and because, according to Barbour, two novelties were first seen therein, which he records as being of equal importance, namely, crests on the helmets of knights and " cracks of war "— that is, cannon.

> Twa novelryis that day tha saw
> That forouth in Scotland had bene nane ;
> Tymbris for helmis was the tane,
> That tham thocht of gret beaute,
> And alsua wondir for to se ;
> The tothir crakis war of wer
> That tha befor herd nevir er.
> Of thir twa thingis tha had ferly.[1]

For a whole month the Scottish army remained in the northern counties. Far smaller in numbers, they successfully evaded pursuit by Edward's heavier columns ; but many feats of arms were done between detached parties of either army. The object of the English was to intercept the Scots in their northward retreat, and so far they were completely successful. Finally, at the beginning of August, the two armies lay facing each other upon opposite banks of the Wear at Stanhope. The English occupied the north bank, and it seemed as if they held their weaker enemy at their mercy.

[1] Barbour's *Brus*, cxli. 170-177.

But twenty years of Border war had made
Douglas and Moray very slippery to hold. On
4th August they caused a great show of preparation to be made in their camp, and purposely
allowed a Scottish soldier to be captured, in
order that he might make them believe that
a night attack had been ordered. This kept
the English under arms all night. In the
morning, two trumpeters that Douglas had left
to blow deceptive calls in the darkness, were
brought in prisoners to the English camp;
when it was found that the Scots had given
their enemy the slip, had marched round their
flank during the night, and were already miles
on the way to the Border. Young King
Edward wept tears of chagrin at this issue of
his mighty preparations, and disbanded his
army at York on 15th August. He should
not have been so precipitate. King Robert
was accustomed to act according to an
axiom to be formulated later by a Frenchman.
*En guerre, l'art ne consiste pas à frapper fort,
ni à frapper souvent, mais à frapper juste.* In
war the secret is, not to strike hard, nor to

strike often, so much as to strike at the right moment.

Within three weeks of the dismissal of the English army, three separate columns of Scots were over the Border again, and where they went they left little of value behind them. King Robert himself led one of these columns —his last appearance on active service. For, after the people of Northumberland and Durham had purchased from him a truce to last till Pentecost, 1328, lo! there came an embassy from the parliament at Lincoln with proposals for the marriage of King Edward's sister Joanna to Prince David the heir of Scotland.

Of course this meant peace—such peace as King Robert had always been ready to accept —peace with honour. It meant that for which torrents of blood had flowed—that for which many gallant Scottish knights had suffered on the scaffold—that for which thousands of homesteads had been given to the flames— that for which the industry and commerce of both countries had been squandered for more than a generation. It meant that, at the moment when it was least looked for, the independence of Scotland was to be admitted and confirmed by the only government that disputed it ; that the Scottish people were at length to gain the management of their own affairs without foreign interference. The whole weary, wasteful controversy, which, but for the resolute devotion of the slaughtered Wallace, might have gone by default against the nation more than thirty years before, was about to be laid to rest for ever.

Commissioners were appointed at once, and, meeting at Newcastle on 1st March, 1328, received King Edward's assurance, embodied forthwith in an indenture, that he abandoned for himself and his heirs all claim to supremacy or overlordship over Scotland, and that all writings which might have a contrary purport should be void and of no effect.

Treaty of Northampton, 4th May, 1328. This indenture was submitted to the English parliament sitting at Northampton in May, and its provisions were embodied in a treaty of perpetual peace, confirmed by royal charters.

172

TREATY OF NORTHAMPTON

The Scottish duplicate of the indenture and King Edward's charter, both of them in French, may be seen in the General Register Office, Edinburgh.

It is to be noted that no mention is made in these documents of the restoration to Scotland of the Coronation Stone of Scone. Nevertheless, that was not overlooked, for King Edward issued his writ to the Dean and Chapter of Westminster, bidding them deliver the stone to the Sheriffs of London ; no doubt intending that it should be returned to Scotland. But, as the Lanercost chronicler affirms, the people of London would not consent to its removal ; and, as is well known to you all, it remains where it was placed by the first and greatest Edward, Hammer of the Scots, under the seat of the throne in Westminster Abbey ; nor need we now grudge the people of London the custody thereof, seeing that since 1603, when the English had to come to Scotland for a king, the Stone of Destiny has justified its designation by providing a seat for successive monarchs of the united realm.

The startling suddenness with which the English claim of supremacy was abandoned and formal recognition made of Robert the Bruce's kingship and dynasty, did much to deepen the displeasure of the English people with the Queen mother, Isabella, and her paramour, Mortimer, who virtually ruled the country during Edward's minority. The motive of their precipitancy is obvious. As Charles King of France died at this time, and as Edward III. claimed to be nearest heir to the crown of France, it was desirable that he should have the Scottish quarrel off his hands before taking the military measures necessary to vindicate his title. And so it came to pass that in the King of England's correspondence you shall no longer find mention of "the rebel Robert de Brus, lately Earl of Carrick," for King Edward now addresses himself to his dearest friend "the magnificent Prince Sir Robert, by the grace of God King of Scots, greeting and embraces of sincere affection." (9th August, 1328.)

It is true that in official documents of this

date not intended for Scottish inspection the language used was the reverse of complimentary to the royal house of Scotland. Thus, on 18th December, 1328, that clerk must have thoroughly enjoyed a privy satisfaction who engrossed a deed conveying to a certain knight lands in Ireland forfeited by another knight for his rebellion " in company of Robert de Brus, Edward de Brus and other Scottish felons."

The marriage of the two children—Prince David of Scotland, aged four, and Princess Joan of England, aged six—was celebrated with great rejoicings at Berwick—a city of grim association—on 12th July, 1328.

David of Scotland marries Joan of England, 12th July, 1328.

King Robert was unable to be present at this most auspicious wedding. Although only in his fifty-fifth year, the rigours of his early adventures had permanently undermined his health ; his life-work had been accomplished and now, as Froissart puts it, " there was no way for him but death." He died on 7th June, 1329.

Death of the King of Scots, 7th June, 1329.

In the sketch which I have endeavoured to give you of him to whose resolute will and

strong arm the Scottish nation owes its very
existence, I have said nothing to palliate or
condone Robert Bruce's desertion of Wallace,
his manifold treason to Edward I., the brutal
murder of his brother knight in Greyfriars
Church. Yet we have it on good authority
that there is more joy over one sinner that
repenteth, etc. Judge him by the standard of
this or that or any other age, his character as a
young knight must be deemed as deeply stained;
but from the moment that the Countess of Fife
placed the kingly diadem on his brow, he
followed a single purpose with unwavering integrity, dauntless courage and consummate
sagacity. The extraordinary fidelity with which
he was served was all the more remarkable
when we consider the experience of his successors on the throne. No doubt this was owing
in great measure to King Robert's personal
charm of manner, and his ready sympathy with
men of every degree.

In all history I know of no more striking
group of three than Robert Bruce, James
Douglas and Randolph Moray. Their joint

memory is the priceless heritage of all Scotsmen; were pilgrimages still the manner whereby reverence to such memories is paid, then surely the tombs of these three stalwarts would be more highly honoured than other shrines. At least it might have been expected of the Scottish nation, which owes its very existence to the bold heart, the wise head and the strong arm of Robert the Bruce, that they would have guarded his last resting-place with ceaseless vigilance. His body was laid under a costly marble canopy, made in Paris, in the choir of Dunfermline Abbey, reckoned at that time the most sacred spot in all Scotland; for when the different races inhabiting that country united to form one nation under one monarch, Dunfermline succeeded Iona as the sepulchre of the Scottish kings. Here had been laid Malcolm Canmore, his sainted Queen Margaret and their three sons, Edward, Edmund and Ethelbert; Alexander I. "the Fierce" and his Queen Sibylla; David I. and his Queen Matilda; Alexander III. and his Queen Margaret, with their two sons, David and Alexander.

DISMISSAL OF THE BALLIOLS

Even were there to be found a Scot so alien in spirit from his race as to hold the memory of Robert the Bruce of small account; or one who held that royal ashes deserved no more reverence than those of other men, even to him the ground at Dunfermline should be as deeply hallowed as Westminster Abbey is to Englishmen; for thither, in the centuries following the reign of our first Robert, were brought the remains of many that Scotland cherished as wise and great and good among her sons. Surely the place would be held sacred for all time; surely, in all the coming virulence of faction and bitterness of ecclesiastical strife, the marble memorial set over our great king should have been proudly protected.

Desecration of King Robert's tomb, 1560. It was not to be. To our shame be it said, it was not to be. On 28th March, 1560, the choir, transepts and belfry, as well as the monastery of Dunfermline, were razed to the ground by the Reformers, and four years later the nave was refitted to serve as a parish kirk. Ruin—ruthless, senseless ruin—fell upon the monument of Scotland's greatest ruler, just as about that time it fell upon countless other relics of priceless value. And so it came to pass in 1821, when the foundations were being cleared for a new church, no man could point with certainty to the place where King Robert had been laid. A grave was found, indeed, near the site of the high altar, and in it was the skeleton of a man, the breast-bone having been sawn across as if for the removal of the heart. The skull was there—was it the same that the great Plantagenet had so eagerly desired to see fixed upon London Bridge? Probably. There is a cast of it in the Scottish Antiquaries' Museum in Edinburgh, and with it some fragments of fine linen threaded with gold which lay about the bones, as well as shattered morsels of black and white marble, carved and guilt, all that remains of the Paris sculptor's handiwork. By so much as we have failed as a nation in pre-serving the perishable relics of the saviour of our independence, is the obligation upon us more urgent to keep fresh the memory of his life's work.

We are not likely to forget the picturesque

and dramatic episodes in his career—the dark affair in Greyfriars Church, Dumfries—the coronation at Scone—the hairbreadth escapes in the Highland wanderings and the glens of Galloway—the crowning triumph of Bannock-burn; but we are not unlikely to overlook King Robert's work as a civil ruler, the impress whereof remains upon the national character and institutions to this day.

Rise of the Scottish burghs.

Although the burghs of Scotland had attained considerable wealth and influence under David I. and Alexander III., King Robert was the first to admit them to representation in parliament at the Cambuskenneth session of 1326. At no time do we find in Scotland that which is such a conspicuous feature in the early history of some other countries, namely, jealousy and discord between urban communities and the feudal owners of the soil. The code of chivalry was as scrupulously honoured by the Scottish barons as in any other kingdom, but it never prevailed to raise the cold barrier of caste between the seigneury and the burgesses. The cadets of noble and knightly families were not

held to degrade their rank if they engaged in
trade, and successful merchants often became
the founders of noble families. It is almost
certain, for instance, that the great houses of
Douglas and Moray owned a common descent
from a wealthy Flemish trader Freskin, upon
whom David I. settled extensive lands in the
conquered province of Moray. The Scottish
burghs in particular, and the kingdom of Scotland in general, derived immense benefit from
the wise policy of the kings, who, when
Henry II. drove all foreigners out of England,
encouraged those industrious traders and skilled
mechanics, the Flemings, to settle in the
northern realm.

The relations between the feudal and burghal
magnates in Scotland during the twelfth,
thirteenth and fourteenth centuries have been
aptly compared to those prevailing in the
republics of Genoa and Venice; and King
Robert, albeit by birth and association a Norman
baron, did much to foster the system.

Unluckily, at the time when peaceful relations between England and Scotland ended

with the reign of John Balliol, Berwick, the wealthiest and busiest town in Scotland, was most exposed to loss in war with England. Some idea of the volume of trade in that seaport may be gathered from the fact that the customs of Berwick were accepted by a Gascon merchant as security for a debt of £2197 due by Alexander III. for corn and wine, and this at a time when the whole customs of England amounted to only £8411.

Talking of customs duties, it is necessary to remind you that these were not in Scotland part of the royal revenue, but consisted of the *parva costuma* levied by each burgh on all produce, whether foreign or native, coming within its boundary. The fiscal policy of the Scottish government affords the earliest authentic example of free trade. No duty was levied upon imported goods, and this policy continued in force till 1597, when an Act was passed imposing a duty upon cloth and other manufactures. The object of that new departure was not, as you might suppose, the patriotic one of protecting home industries, but, as set forth in the preamble of the Act, the far less worthy one of enabling King James VI. to acquire funds "for the enterteyning of his princely port." Allusion is made in the same preamble to the immemorial exemption from duty of all imports into Scotland, which is shown to be contrary to the practice of all other nations. The Convention of Royal Burghs remonstrated strongly against this measure, which they declared imposed "ane new and intollerabill custome."

It is difficult to reconcile with this policy of free imports the heavy duties exacted under Robert I. on the exportation of wool and hides. In our own day we have seen 1s. a ton on coal exports denounced and abandoned as irreconcilable with free trade principles.

As a Galloway man, I cannot refrain from noticing an Act passed by King Robert's parliament of Glasgow in 1324, whereby it was enacted that any Gallovidian charged with an offence had the option of trial by jury, instead of submitting to the old code of ordeal by battle.

It is well known that, at the time of the union

with England, the Scottish coinage had been so grievously debased that since early in the seventeenth century the Scottish pound was only one-twelfth of the value of the English. It is not uncommonly supposed that the depreciation began in the reign of Robert I. This is not so. King Robert not only won his kingdom, but he maintained and increased its prosperity. It was not until 1355, twenty-six years after his death, that the Scottish government adopted the vicious precedent of their French allies and attempted to meet their necessities by debasing the currency.

The disinherited lords, 1330-32.

Well, Robert the Bruce left to his people an independent kingdom of Scotland, but he also left them exposed to the disquietude arising from a long minority in the person of his successor, David II., who came to the throne at the age of five, his Queen, Joan of England —of the Tower, being aged seven. The Black Douglas had perished in fulfilling his master's commission to carry his heart to the Holy Land. Randolph Moray, last of the trio, was a capable regent, but he failed to carry out that part of the treaty of Northampton which provided for the reinstatement of certain English barons in their Scottish possessions. There were three of these disinherited lords, Wake, Lord of Liddel; Beaumont, Earl of Buchan; and Henry, Lord Percy. Their lands had been forfeited by King Robert and bestowed upon his own adherents. It cannot have been easy for Moray to dispossess the new owners in favour of Englishmen; such a proceeding would be too likely to bring about civil war. He did manage to reinstate Percy, but by failing to satisfy the perfectly just demands of the other two, he went near to forfeiting the hard won independence of his country. In 1330 King Edward demanded of his brother-in-law, King David, who had now attained the ripe age of six, the fulfilment of the treaty of Northampton. To add force to the claim, he brought back to England Edward Balliol, son and heir of the dethroned John. Regent Moray would not or could not comply, and when the demand was repeated in 1332, King Edward looked another way while the disinherited lords landed an invading force in Fife, bringing Edward Balliol as a pretender to the throne. Just at that time Regent Moray died, and was succeeded in the regency by the Earl of Mar, nephew of the deceased King Robert. Mar proved a futile leader, whether in the council or the field. Despising the Fabian strategy which the Bruce had consistently observed with such brilliant result, he attacked Balliol's army where it was strongly posted near Dupplin, and paid for his error by a bloody defeat and his own life. The English archery fire was more than the Scottish pikemen could endure.

Death of Randolph Moray, 20th July, 1332.

This was on 12th August: on 24th September, Edward Balliol was crowned King of Scots at Scone, the Earl of Fife, who had been taken prisoner at Dupplin, discharging his hereditary function of placing the diadem on his brow, just as his sister Isabel had done to the Bruce a quarter of a century before. Then Edward Balliol hurried off to Roxburgh to do homage to another and greater Edward as his over-

Edward Balliol crowned at Scone, 24th September, 1332.

lord and suzerain, and to hand over to him the town and castle of Berwick. The whole of Robert Bruce's work seemed to lie in ruins —independence a brilliant dream of the past. Nay, but never had any dream the substance and reality of this. There were still leal hearts and strong arms in Scotland. Good Sir James —the Black Douglas—was no more ; but his youngest brother, Archibald, was of the same mettle and mould. The earth had but lately received gallant Randolph Moray to rest, his eldest son had fallen at Dupplin, but his second son was now third Earl of Moray, and breathed a like spirit as the others. These two, Archibald Douglas and young Earl Moray, having bold Simon Fraser in company, tracked Balliol from Roxburgh to Annan, and there, on a dark December night, surprised his household, slew some of them, and hunted the would-be king in his shirt-tails to shelter at Carlisle. Wyntoun describes this camisade pithily.

The camisade of Annan, Christmas, 1332.

> " Bot the Ballyoll his gat is gane
>   On a barme hors wyth leggis bare ;
>   Swa fell that he eth chapped thare.

> The lave, that ware noucht tane in hand,
> Fled qwhare thai mycht fynd warrand ;
> Swa that all that cumpany
> Dyscumfyt ware all halyly." [1]

I desire here to enter a strong protest against the designation given to Edward Balliol in that excellent work the *Dictionary of National Biography*, where he is described as King of Scotland. In the first place, there never was a King of Scotland before the union with England. The true and significant style of the monarch was ever " King of Scots." In the second place, David II. had neither abdicated nor been dethroned, how then could there be a second king upon his throne ? There never was an Edward King of Scots until the accession of our late king on 22nd January, 1901.

However, Scotland was not yet rid of the Balliols. If Edward Balliol left the realm in unseemly disarray by the western border, he returned in six months by the eastern border at the head of an English army. Edward III. had thrown off all disguise ; he was now at open war

---

[1] Wyntoun's *Cronykil,* Book viii. ch. 26.

with the government of his brother-in-law, King David, and the treaty of Northampton lay in shreds. Archibald Douglas "the Tyneman" had become Regent of Scotland, and repeated with singular fidelity the fatal blunders of his predecessor Mar. Just as Mar had given Balliol the chance of a pitched battle at Dupplin, and not only lost that field, but his own life and the lives of many chief officers, so on 19th July, 1333, did Douglas attack Balliol and the English army at Halidon Hill, near Berwick, and perished with five Scottish earls and a great number of barons, knights, and rank and file.

Battle of Halidon Hill, 19th July, 1333.

The blow was crushing; by a nation of softer material than the Scots it might well have been accepted as final, for the Scottish realm was dismembered. Berwick was surrendered to the English, and Edward Balliol, who had already acknowledged English Edward as his overlord, was now forced to cede to him as the price of aid rendered, the three Lothians and the counties of Roxburgh, Peebles, Dumfries, and Kirkcudbright to remain for ever part of the English realm. But if we are to learn one thing more clearly than anything else from the history of our country, it is this—although a strong man may lead Scotsmen in any direction, and as far as men may go, they will not be driven.

Among the few who escaped from Halidon Hill were Robert Stewart, grandson of the Bruce, and afterwards first of the Stuart kings, and young Randolph, Earl of Moray. Their first care was for the boy King David. Him they sent to France for safety, and then bestirred themselves to organise the patriot party.

Edward III. lays Scotland waste, 1335. Edward III. unconsciously did his best to promote resistance to his rule and his puppet Balliol's by a devastating invasion with which he ravaged the land in the summer of 1335. In the course of a couple of years after this the English had incurred so deep a hatred from the unhappy people of Scotland, that in 1337, when Edward again directed his attention to pressing his claim to the throne of France, the tide turned, and a long series of successes rewarded the fidelity of the patriots to their absent king. The castles of Perth, Stirling, Edinburgh and

Roxburgh were captured in succession ; so that in 1341 it was considered safe to bring King David, eighteen years old by this time, back to his kingdom. They had done better to have left him where he was ; for although he would have been safe enough in bonny Scotland, he was not content to remain within his own marches, drawn as those marches had been by the usurper Balliol to exclude David from a great part of his rightful heritage. Is he to be blamed for rashness in taking advantage of King Edward's preoccupation in France and making a gallant assault upon the territory that Balliol had bartered away. Nay, but had he been a few years older, he might have acted more wisely than he did, and refrained from invading what was undoubtedly English realm. He recovered Liddesdale—good ; he pushed on into England—not so good ; for, after a successful raid in the old manner, he found Lord Percy and the Archbishop of York posted on strong ground at Neville's Cross near Durham. He was strongly advised by William Douglas, known then as the Flower of Chivalry, later as the Knight of Liddesdale,

Battle of Neville's Cross, 17th October, 1346.

to avoid an encounter and to return home quietly with his booty. David was too young to have taken to heart the lesson of Halidon Hill. Turn aside from these " miserable monks and pig-drivers," as he called them ? Not he. He attacked them hotly and paid for it in exactly the same manner as the Scots had paid at Halidon Hill. The English archery fire, here as there, proved intolerable. The flower of the Scottish nobility fell thickly round their king ; the young Earl of Moray, last of his line, Keith, Earl Marischal and more than thirty barons. King David himself was taken prisoner with the Knight of Liddesdale and many others, and there was unhappy Scotland once more leaderless, and the cause of her independence hopeless, one would say. So, at least, thought the Knight of Liddesdale, who entered into treasonable dealings with the English government to secure his own lands and liberty, thereby forging the first link in the long chain of treachery and crime which goes so far to outweigh the earlier virtues of the House of Douglas.

WILLIAM DOUGLAS

But there was another and a younger Douglas who was to redeem his country from her low estate, namely, William, younger son of Regent Archibald, who, at the time of these events, was finishing his education in France. The battle of Neville's Cross was fought on 17th October, 1346. Young William Douglas, returning to Scotland shortly afterwards, found that neither Edward Balliol nor Edward of England were in a position to take advantage of that great victory. English Edward, indeed, was engaged on the campaign of Crecy at the time. To quote the account given by a contemporary chronicler :

"In the mean whyle that King Davy was prisoner, the lords of Scotland, by a litle and a litle, wan all that they had lost at the bataille of Duresme ; and there was much envy emong them who might be hyest; for every one rulid yn hys owne cuntery ; and King Eduarde was so distressid with his afferes beyound the se, that he toke litle regard to the Scottische matiers."

Young William Douglas, therefore (who afterwards became first Earl of Douglas), bestirred himself with great success in expelling the English from his hereditary lands in

William, Lord of Douglas, 1327 (?)– 1384.

Douglasdale and Ettrickdale. The Scots were ever ready to rally to a strong man in a good cause; and so it came to pass in 1347 that King Edward, having taken Calais, was forced to conclude a truce with the King of France, which truce was prolonged till 1354. As it included the Scots as allies of the French, we may acknowledge that here once more the Scoto-French alliance saved the independence of Scotland.

But the mere alliance could not have saved it without the staunch fidelity with which the Scots—nobles, knights and people—upheld the cause of their king during his long imprisonment in England. A new spirit had been born in Scotland. As Mr. Andrew Lang has justly observed, when the Scottish parliament of Arbroath sent their famous and defiant letter to the Pope in 1320, they were animated by the enthusiasm inspired by such a leader as King Robert and by personal devotion to him, rather than by the spontaneous patriotism which binds together men sprung from a common soil. But before the fourteenth cen-

194

tury had run half its course, the long ordeal of war had welded all parts of Scotland into a solid realm, and kindled in the various races that peopled it a fervid devotion to the country as well as to the crown. Edward Balliol was an abler man and better soldier than his father, John ; but his only strength lay in the support of the disinherited lords and in the adherence of the native lords of eastern Galloway, where was his father's estate of Buittle. But he never obtained any hold over the affection of the people, and when his supporters fell out among themselves over the disposition of the lands, his cause began to wane, until even Edward III. wearied of him whom he styled on paper "our dear cousin Edward, King of Scotland." His disappearance from public life was not more dignified than that of his father, King John. It came about in this way. David II. was released from imprisonment in 1354 under treaty providing for a truce that was to include Edward Balliol, and a payment as ransom of 90,000 marks, to be spread over nine years. But only one instalment of the ransom was paid. It did not suit the French King John that England should be at peace with Scotland for nine years, so he sent over some knights and troops with 40,000 *moutons d'or* as sinews of war, and the time-honoured game of raid and counter-raid was renewed. As the instalment of ransom due for 1355 was not forthcoming, King David returned to prison in England, apparently a scrupulously honourable proceeding, but, as will be shown presently, kingly honour was not one of David's attributes, and a liking for the luxurious English court was so.

Dismissal of Edward Balliol, 25th January, 1356.

King Edward now resolved to be done with the futile Balliol. At Roxburgh, on 25th January, 1356, he received from him the golden diadem and a sod of Scottish soil in token of his absolute and final renunciation of all claim to the crown. Aged and childless, Edward Balliol retired on a pension of £2000 a year from the English king, and disappeared from the scene for ever—unwept, unhonoured and unsung.

It remained for King Edward to reduce the

Scottish people to his will, a task which the magnificent army which he had assembled at Roxburgh seemed to render very simple to the victor of Crecy. But the Scots had now a leader of the right stamp.

William, Lord of Douglas, was sent by Regent Robert Stewart to negotiate with King Edward at Roxburgh. He proved himself an adept in diplomacy. In order that the regent might have time for preparation, Douglas wasted ten of King Edward's precious days in making absolutely fictitious proposals. When at last the English army did advance, they found the country a desert before them. The Scots had reverted to the safe strategy of Robert the Bruce, namely, avoiding battle and wasting the land in the line of the enemy's march. King Edward pushed forward as far as Edinburgh, trusting to meet his victualling fleet in the Forth; but a storm had scattered the convoy, so he was forced to beat a retreat in order to avoid starvation, venting his chagrin in burning churches and houses to an extent remarkable even in those days, so that the

The Burnt Candlemas, 1356.

197

spring of 1356 was known ever after as the "Burnt Candlemas." Among other damage which we have cause to deplore to this day was the destruction of the Lamp of Lothian—the beautiful Abbey Church of Haddington.[1] Douglas, like his uncle, the Good Sir James, was an expert in ambuscade, and came very near capturing Edward himself near Melrose. It would have been a strange situation had the Kings of Scotland and England been prisoners simultaneously in the country of each other. As it was, the proud array of the English recrossed the Border in appearance very different from that in which they had left it, and thus was foiled the last attempt of three successive Plantagenet kings to bend to their will the nation of which they claimed to be overlords.

Release of King David, 3rd October, 1357.

King Edward was no sooner back in London than he made up his mind to give up the Scottish quarrel and concentrate his energy

---

[1] Not, probably, the Church of Our Lady, still used in part as the parish church, and, by the nobility of its architecture, well entitled to be styled *Lucerna Laudoniæ*. The real "Lamp of Lothian," the church of the Franciscans, was lower down the river.

upon the French war. A truce was arranged on 25th March, 1357, to endure till Michaelmas ; on 3rd October King David's eleven years of captivity came to an end ; the price exacted from the Scots for receiving back their worthless king being 100,000 marks, to be paid in ten yearly instalments. Aye, he was worthless —far worse than worthless—this ignoble David who had cost his countrymen so dear already, and whose ransom was to press so sorely upon them and their children. This degenerate son of the Bruce had ceased to be a Scot, save in name. Body and soul he had sold himself to England. Three great lords and twenty Scottish youths of noble birth went into exile as hostages for payment of the ransom, little knowing that David had already done homage in secret to King Edward of England for his kingdom.

Far better had it been for Scotland and her people had King David been left, nominally a prisoner, at his brother-in-law's court. Better financially, for the burden of his ransom, added to the obligation to defray the charges of the hostages, brought the nation to the verge of bankruptcy : better politically, for the government was safer in the hands of Regent Stewart than in those of a spendthrift king to whom the years of manhood had brought no increment of understanding or common sense.

It was not long before the loyal Scots found out what a shocking bad bargain they had made. King David showed no gratitude towards Robert Stewart, who had administered the realm courageously and wisely during David's captivity. David was childless; therefore, not unnaturally perhaps, jealous of Robert, his heir-presumptive, who had a large family by his two wives. Things came to such a pass that in the spring of 1363 Robert Stewart, Douglas, March and others banded themselves together in protest against the king's extravagance. To raise money for his ransom, he had become a wool-jobber. All the wool of the country was "thirled" to him at a fixed price, and that a low one; he then sold it in the dearest market. No objection was raised against this on economic grounds : but when the king, instead of applying the profits to payment of the ransom, squandered them on his own pleasures, then his barons entered strong and threatening protest. David managed to put down what was virtually an insurrection, but it still required the utmost vigilance on the part of his council and parliament to prevent him making a surrender even more ignominious than Balliol's. He was ready to hand over the crown of Scotland to King Edward at any moment; but to Edward, wanting funds for the war in France, regular payment of the ransom was far more important than a heritage which he had learnt by experience was so thorny.

Nevertheless, Edward expressed himself willing to remit the ransom altogether in consideration of settling the succession of Scotland upon his younger son Lionel, in the event of David's death without issue. David actually had the hardihood to propose this to the parliament of Scone in March, 1364, but the mere suggestion was indignantly scouted by the estates in the same spirit which dictated the letter to the Pope in 1320. You remember the words:

DISMISSAL OF THE BALLIOLS

" Should our king abandon our cause, or aim at reducing us or our kingdom under the dominion of the English, we will instantly strive to expel him as a common enemy . . . and we will choose another king to rule over us : for, *while there exist a hundred of us, we will never submit to England.*"

King David's treachery.

Nevertheless, never was the cause of independence in greater jeopardy than it was at this time. Betrayed as they had been by their king, the people of Scotland must have been more than human had they not groaned under the new taxation, whence relief could have been had by delivering the succession to England. Even had they remained staunch in their resolve, never to let an Englishman reign over them, where were the means to resume the war which seemed the only alternative to submission? Their resources had been drained to the uttermost.

Once again the French alliance saved the Scottish monarchy. In 1369 King Edward III. proclaimed himself King of France ; to support his claim, withdrew all his fighting force from the Scottish border, and concluded a truce of fourteen years between England and Scotland.

KING DAVID'S TREACHERY

Here we may leave the case. Robert the Bruce had won and established the independence of his country against the will and arms of a large section of the Scottish barons and people : his son, David II., was only withheld from surrendering that independence by the resolute patriotism of the Scottish barons and a united nation.

Centuries of warfare lay before the Scottish people to enable them to hold what had been won, and I propose in the next and closing lecture of this course, not to follow in detail the course of successive campaigns and the tortuous diplomacy of the two courts, but rather to review the general nature of the warfare and its effect upon the character of our people.

VI

THE CHARACTER OF BORDER
WARFARE

VI

IN my last lecture I brought the sketch of
the winning of Scottish independence
down to the point in 1364 when that independence was brought into utmost jeopardy
through the treasonable machination of King
David II.—the unworthy son of Robert the
Bruce—and on to the year 1369, when, not
for the first time nor yet for the last, Scotland was saved by the French alliance, and
the King of England was forced to grant a
truce for fourteen years in order that he might
press his claim to the crown of France.

That truce was very imperfectly kept ; how,
indeed, could Scotsmen tamely submit to see
Annandale and the castles of Lochmaben,
Roxburgh and Berwick remaining in possession
of the English. For more than two hundred
years after that date there were few intervals

in the wasteful war between two nations whose only difference was a political one—a warfare lamentable equally from a moral and economic point of view, yet working such lasting effect on the character, physique and literature of our people as makes it not wholly deplorable.

Instead of asking you to listen to a wearisome chronicle of the course of this warfare, I propose to take a few salient incidents in it, for I should like you to have a clear idea of the kind of life led by your forefathers, and the nature of the difficulties that beset them. Let us first of all realise the fact that from the rise of Robert the Bruce in 1307 until the Union of the Crowns in 1603, a laird might seldom ride abroad without an armed following—a farmer could never leave his cattle in the fields at night—not, at least, within a night's ride of the English border ; and in other parts of Scotland, where the English only came at stated times of invasion, the nobles and lairds generally had a blood feud going among themselves.

What was the cause of it all ?   Why did it

take three centuries for Scots and English
to discover that it was perfectly practicable to
dwell on either side of an imaginary line
without perpetually striving to cut each others
throats. The main industry of the Borders,
then as now, was pastoral and agricultural.
The land was let in farms : why did the
farmers ride about in iron jackets and steel
caps, instead of attending to their peaceable
business. They were probably as anxious to
cultivate their holdings, and mind the markets,
as they are now, but the system was different.
There was very little money rent paid in those
days. Rent was reckoned in kind, so many
nowt, sheep and capons, or so many bolls of
corn were rendered annually to the landlord,
and I have heard farmers in times of low
prices express a wish to revert to that system.
But would they care to adopt the system in
its entirety ? Only part of the rent was paid
in kind. There was no standing army, no
militia or volunteers in those days, and the
most onerous part of the tenant's obligation
was military service. The landowner held his

estate on condition of being ready to bring his tenants into the field whenever the government decided to go to war with England, and interpreted this into license to bring them out whenever he had a dispute with his neighbours.

The first characteristic incident to which I will call your attention rests on the authority of Sir Thomas Gray of Heton, who spent some years of captivity in Edinburgh Castle in writing the annals of his time. And whereas he wrote in Norman French (the common language of both Scots and English knights in those days), it is little known to general readers. The father of the chronicler, also named Sir Thomas Gray, was King Edward's constable of Norham Castle, which he held against the Scots for eleven years. It was about 1316, two years after the battle of Bannockburn, that a number of knights and ladies were assembled at a supper party in a castle in Lincolnshire. Sir William Marmion of Scrivelsby was one of the guests, and during the banquet there was brought to him a helmet with a golden crest—a present from

Marmion's exploit at Norham, c. 1316.

his lady-love. With the gift came a letter
from the lady, bidding him take the helmet
to the most perilous place in Britain, and there
make it famous. Thereupon a discussion
ensued which place best answered to that
description. It was unanimously voted that
there was no place so hazardous as Norham,
for all the other strongholds on the Eastern
Marches, except Alnwick and Bamborough, had
fallen into the hands of the Scots. Thither,
accordingly, hied Sir Marmion, made known
his desires to Sir Thomas Gray, who laughed
and told him he need not fear having long
to wait. Sure enough, just as they were sitting
down to dinner at noon on the fourth day
after his arrival, the alarm was sounded, and
Sir Alexander de Moubray appeared before
the castle with some of the hardiest knights
of the Marches, 160 men-at-arms, and a body
of light horse. The constable was marching
off his men to their posts of defence, when
he saw Sir Marmion straddling across the
courtyard in full armour, with the sun flashing
on his golden helmet. "Ho! Sir Knight,"

cried the constable, "you have come here as
a knight errant to make your helmet famous.
Deeds of chivalry should be done on horseback ;
send for your horse ; see ! there is the foe.
You must spur in among them alone, and I
shall deny my God if I do not rescue you
alive or dead, or die in the attempt." Sir
Marmion sent for his destrier and climbed
into the saddle : the gate of the castle was
swung back, the portcullis raised, the bridge
lowered, and out thundered the knight alone,
and charged straight into the enemy's squadrons.
He was unhorsed at once, and fell badly
wounded ; but stout Sir Thomas Gray was
as good as his word. He led the garrison
on foot to the rescue, and, causing his men
to thrust their spears into the bowels of the
horses, defeated the Scots, who fled pell mell.
Then the women in the castle brought out the
horses to the English soldiers, who hotly pursued
the Scots as far as the outskirts of Berwick,
killing many of them and capturing fifty valuable horses, *chevaux de prix*. Let us hope that
Sir Marmion's lady-love rewarded him, in spite

of his damaged features, for the chronicler says that the Scots *ly naufrerent hu visage*—made a wreck of his face.

Well—in this affair the fortune of war was with the English : but it was not always so. Perhaps one cannot find a more typical and sorrowful instance of the fruitless waste of gallant lives than took place on the night of the 19th and 20th August, 1388. The Scots, under James, second Earl of Douglas, had resolved to beat up Hotspur Percy's quarters at Newcastle, who was known to have just received from France a quantity of valuable armour, including a thousand stand of complete mail. Such a prize was worth an effort, and the greatest secrecy was observed in the plans of the invaders. Douglas is said to have had under his command 30,000 men ; some historians place it at a much higher figure, but no reliance can be placed on the estimates of those days. At the present day, if you wanted to know the strength of the cavalry depot at Canterbury, probably Archbishop Davidson is the last person you would think

The Battle of Otterbourne, 1388.

of consulting, nor if you wished to find out
how many troops composed the garrison of
Edinburgh, would you be likely to trouble the
Very Reverend Sir James Cameron Lees. But
in pre-Reformation times, almost the only
persons capable of compiling a chronicle were
monks and clerics. Well, let the force at his
disposal have been what it may, Douglas divided
it into two; sending the larger moiety under
command of his brother, Sir William Douglas,
to create a diversion by entering England by
way of Carlisle; whilst he himself, with a
chosen body of 400 knights and their followers,
esquires, men-at-arms and 2000 infantry, about
5000 men in all, made a dash for Newcastle.

> "It fell about the Lammas tide,
>   When the muir men win their hay,
> The doughty Douglas bown'd him ride
>   Into England to drive a prey.
>
> "He chose the Gordons and the Graemes,
>   With them the Lindsays, light and gay,
> But the Jardines wald wi' him ride,
>   And they rue it to this day."

The exploit failed; for indeed it was a fool-
hardy thing for a light flying column, not

equipped with siege engines, or even with
scaling ladders, to attempt to capture a walled
town, surrounded by a ditch two-and-twenty
yards wide. But this was the very heyday of
chivalry, so Hotspur rode out from his fortress
to break a lance with doughty Lord Douglas,
who unhorsed him and carried off the pennon
of the English lord's spear.

Finding Newcastle impregnable, Douglas
began his homeward march on the morning
of 14th August, and encamped that night in a
wood on the Otterbourne, a tributary of the
Reedwater, thirty-two miles from Newcastle ;
no trifling performance for cavalry and infantry.
Percy had vowed to recover his pennon ;
Douglas knew that he would be pursued and
his choice of a camping ground is significant.
It was in a wood and he preferred it to a far
stronger position to the north, the old Roman
station of Bremenium, where there were no
trees, because he dreaded the fire of the
English archers. The English were ever better
archers than the Scots : they had longer and
stronger bows, and drew their cloth yard shafts

to the breast, whereas the Scots fired from the hip.

However, as it happened, Percy brought no archers with him. Douglas, who had pledged his word to do him battle, waited four days for his arrival. Percy was too good a soldier to set forth until he had ascertained the movements of the western force under Sir William Douglas. Having satisfied himself of that and made provision for the safety of Newcastle, he set off at noon on 19th August, and reached the banks of the Otter late on the summer evening. His men had marched thirty-two miles, yet he resolved to attack the Scots at once. Detaching a force under Sir Thomas Umfraville to circle round the Scottish position, which consisted of two camps, one containing the cattle and spoil that had been collected, and the baggage under a strong guard; the other, occupied by the main body under Douglas. It was nearly midnight by this time, but there was a brave moon. Percy, unaware of the double nature of the camp, fell upon the baggage enclosure, surprised and slaughtered

the guard, and then found himself confronted by
the main body. Then fighting began in earnest
and lasted all night. At first it went hard with
the Scots, and they began to give way under
superior numbers. A rush was made for the
Douglas standard, and it seemed as if it must
be lost, but Douglas himself, a man of pro-
digious strength, gallantly supported by Sir
Patrick Hepburn and his son, cut his way
through the mellay and turned the tide of
battle.

It was the last act of his life. Bleeding from
three spear wounds, a blow on the head from
Percy's mace brought him to the ground. But
the soldier spirit in him was alive to what was
going on around. Day was just breaking over
the Reedswire; he knew that if his men saw
him dying, the victory which his own prowess
had brought within their reach would be swept
away. The scene is preserved in some of the
most touching stanzas in our ballad literature.

> " My nephew good," the Douglas said,
>   " What recks the death of ane ?
> Last night I dream'd a dreary dream,
>   And I ken the day's thine ain.

BORDER WARFARE

"Last night I dreamed a dreary dream
    Ayont the Isle of Skye;
I saw a dead man win a field
    And I wot that man was I.

"My wound is deep, I fain would sleep;
    Take thou the vanguard of the three,
And hide me by the bracken bush
    That grows on yonder lilye lee.

"O bury me by the bracken bush
    Beneath the blooming brier,
Let never living mortal ken
    That e'er a kindly Scot lies here."

He's lifted up that noble lord,
    Wi' the saut tear in his e'e,
He's hidden him in the bracken bush
    That his merrie men might not see.

The moon was clear, the day drew near,
    The spears in flinders flew,
But many a gallant Englishman
    Ere day the Scotsmen slew.

Douglas fell, but, in fulfilment of this dream,
"the dead man won the field." The English,
be it remembered, had marched thirty-two miles
the previous day; they had fought all night
without resting: human endurance could do no
more, and shortly after sunrise on the 20th the
victorious Scots were pressing their foes before

them, as they forced their way to the north, carrying with them as prisoners Hotspur Percy and his brother.

The ballad from which I have quoted retains a pathetic interest for us for the following reason. When, broken in fortune and shattered in health, Sir Walter Scott was writing *Castle Dangerous*, he travelled with Lockhart to visit Douglas Castle, where he intended to lay the scene. We are told that as he stood mutely gazing at that place of crowded association, the tears came into his eyes and that, striking his stick into the sod, he turned slowly away, repeating the lines—

> My wound is deep, I fain would sleep ;
> Take thou the vanguard of the three,
> And hide me by the bracken bush
> That grows on yonder lilye lee.
>
> O bury me by the bracken bush
> Beneath the blooming brier,
> Let never living mortal ken
> That e'er a kindly Scot lies here.

Now the battle of Otterbourne was bloody and fierce enough, God wot ! yet not more bloody and fierce than a hundred others of which the

memory has passed away. What was there to
cause it to be specially commemorated in the
Scottish ballad which I have just quoted, and
also in the English ballad of *Chevy Chase*? It
was the fate of the two leaders, the death of
Douglas and the capture of Percy, and you will

*The cruelty
of medieval
war.*

not grasp the real cruelty of this warfare, in
spite of the romance that has been thrown round
it, unless you realise the significance of that.
In medieval warfare, before the invention of
gunpowder, the common soldiers and the farmers
and peasants who followed their lords to the
field, counted only as pawns in the game. The
object was to kill as many of them as possible,
prisoners being costly and troublesome. But
the barons, knights, and esquires were regarded
very differently. They rode into battle with
charmed lives, and it was only in exceptional
disasters, such as Bannockburn on the one side,
or Flodden on the other, that any large number
were slain. The great object was to take these
gentlemen of coat-armour prisoners, and hold
them to ransom. A landed proprietor's farms
might be burned and the live stock driven off;

his ruined tenants might be unable to pay any rent; but let him have the good fortune to capture some person of distinction on the other side, and he would recoup himself for all loss. That, as well as the love of adventure, was what kept the game of war so long alive between two nations, which subsequent history has shown are well able to dwell together in amity. It was a huge gambling transaction, with all the excitement of high play, *plus* that of brigandage and military glory. But you will see how cruelly it pressed on the peasantry who had nothing to gain but all to lose. Gunpowder, which at first seemed likely to make war more horrible than before, was really a merciful invention; it not only rendered battles less bloody, but it cured barons and knights of their intense passion for war, because a bullet was as likely to find its billet in the carcase of a noble as in that of a churl.

Does anybody want to know what kind of troops they were that maintained for so long such an unequal contest? Well, they were not very splendid in appearance. Froissart has left a very minute description of the Scottish border riders before the invention of gunpowder altered their equipment, and it enables us to understand how they were able to accomplish such immense distances in a short time. Like our brave enemy in the South African war, their distinguishing quality was extraordinary mobility. He thus describes the equipment of those who marched with Douglas and Moray into Weardale in 1327 —sixty years before the battle of Otterbourne :

"The Scots are bold, hardy and much inured to war. When they make their invasions into England they march from twenty to four-and-twenty miles without halting, as well by night as day—for they are all on horseback, except the camp followers, who are on foot. The knights and squires are well mounted on large bay horses, the common people on little Galloways. They bring no carriages with them, on account of the mountains they have to pass in Northumberland : neither do they convey with them any provision of bread or wine, for their habits of sobriety are such in time of war that they will live a long time on flesh half-sodden, and drink the water of the river without wine. They have, therefore, no occasion for pots and pans, for they dress the flesh of their cattle in the skins ; and, being sure to find plenty of cattle in the country which they invade, they carry none with them. Under the flap of the saddle each man carries a broad plate of metal ; behind the saddle a little bag of oatmeal. When they have eaten too much of the sodden flesh, and their stomachs appear weak and empty, they place this plate over the fire, mix water with their oatmeal, and when the plate is heated, they put a little of the paste upon it, and make a thin cake like a biscuit, which they eat to warm their stomachs. It is, therefore, no wonder that they perform a longer day's march than other soldiers. In this manner the Scots entered England, destroying and burning everything as they passed."

Set against this account of the Scottish troops what Holinshed tells us of the English soldiers whom they defeated in this campaign at Biland, and it is not difficult to realise what led the Scots in later years to nickname their hereditary foes the "pock-puddings." Only you will understand please, that these were troops drawn from the southern counties by Edward III., not the English border riders, who were just as hardy as the Scots.

Holinshed's description of an English army.

"Bicause," says Holinshed, "the English soldiers of this armie were cloathed all in cotes and hoods embroidered with floweres and branches verie seemlie, and vsed to nurish their beards, the Scots in derision thereof made a rime, which they fastened vpon the church doores of Saint Peter-toward-Stangate, containing this that followeth :

> Longe beardes, hartelesse,
> Paynted hoods, witlesses,
> Gaie cotes, gracelesse,
> Make Englande, thriftlesse."

These gay coats were the liveries of the great feudal barons, with whom it was a point of honour to excel in the splendour of their retinues. But many years of enforced economy had taught the Scottish lords to despise, or at least to dispense with, such magnificence.

Rout of
Solway
Moss,
1542.

The easiest victory the English ever had was at the battle of Solway Moss in 1542, when James V., having quarrelled with his nobles, sent them out to meet the army of Henry VIII. under the Duke of Norfolk. James had appointed Oliver Sinclair, an ordinary gentleman of cloak and sword, to command these proud barons. Too sore in spirit to fight, too proud to fly, they allowed themselves to be taken prisoners, and two hundred of them went into captivity in England, where they were held to ransom ; a terrible drain on the resources of their sadly impoverished country. Three weeks later James died of a broken heart, leaving his distracted kingdom to the evils of another regency.

Yet this James, father of Mary Queen of Scots, was far from being an indolent ruler.

Not only was he vigilant and successful in maintaining the integrity of his realm from English invasion, but early in his reign he took vigorous measures to put down moss-trooping, and, during the brief periods of truce, directed his Wardens of the Marches to co-operate with the English wardens to the same end. There was a tract of country about ten miles square at the mouth of the Solway known as the Debatable or Thriep Lands, which belonged to neither country and was claimed by both. Now, it is easy to imagine how, after two centuries of border warfare, there were plenty of men, naturally honest, but deprived of the means of an honest livelihood by the loss of all their gear, and driven to moss-trooping as the only means of maintaining existence. These congregated in the Debatable Lands which became a perfect hive of brigandage. In June, 1530, the young King James made a determined effort to settle the Debatable Lands, and his expedition furnished the theme of one of our most touching ballads. He began by taking the precaution of imprisoning Lords Bothwell,

BORDER WARFARE

Maxwell, Home, Walter Scott of Buccleuch, and other border lairds, who, in the words of Sir James Balfour, "had winked at the willanies" of the Armstrongs, Elliots, Grahams, Nixons, Olivers, Irvings, Bells, Dicksons, Littles, and other noted moss-troopers. The most noted among them at this time was Johnnie Armstrong of Gilnockie, whom King James summoned before him on arriving in Teviotdale. It is said that a royal proclamation had been issued to the effect that the lives of all broken men should be spared, who would come forward and make submission to the king. But, alas for kingly honour! The Armstrongs and their accomplices had been excommunicated, and all men were absolved from keeping faith with them. It had been more to his renown had King James employed his army of 8000 men (Pitscottie says 12,000) in harrying the robber's nest. Howbeit, Gilnockie rode into the king's camp openly with a following of four-and-twenty well equipped horsemen. "What wants yon knave that a king should have?" exclaimed the angry king. Gilnockie protested that he had

James V. and Johnnie Armstrong.

JOHNNIE ARMSTRONG

never injured any but Englishmen, and under-
took to bring in any Englishman, alive or dead,
whom the king should name, within a given day.

"May I find grace, my sovereign liege,
 Grace for my loyal men and me?
For my name it is Johnie Armstrang,
 And subject of yours, my liege," said he.

"Away, away, thou traitor strang!
 Out o' my sicht sune mays't thou be!
I grantit never a traitor's life,
 And now I'll not begin with thee."

"Grant me my life, my liege, my king!
 And a goodly gift I'll gie to thee;
Full four-and-twenty milk-white steeds,
 Were a' foaled in a year to me.

"I'll gie thee a' these milk-white steeds,
 That prance and nicher at a spear,
Wi' as meikle gude English gelt
 As four o' their braid backs can bear."

"Away, away, thou traitor strang!" *etc., etc.*

"Grant me my life, my liege, my king!
 And a costly gift I'll gie to thee;
Gude four-and-twenty ganging mills,
 That gang through a' the year to me.

"These four-and-twenty mills compleat
 Sall gang for thee thro' a' the year;
And as meikle o' gude red wheat
 As a' their happers dow to bear."

BORDER WARFARE

"Away, away, thou traitor strang!" *etc., etc.*

"Grant me my life, my liege, my king!
　And a great gift I'll gie to thee;
Bauld four-and-twenty sisters' sons
　Sall for thee fecht, tho' a' suld flee.

"Grant me my life, my liege, my king,
　And a brave gift I'll give to thee—
All between here and Newcastle town
　Sall pay their yearly rent to thee."

"Away, away, thou traitor strang!
　Out o' my sicht thou mayest sune be,
I grantit never a traitor's lyfe,
　And now I'll not begin with thee."

"Ye lied, ye lied, now king!" he says,
　"Althocht a king and prince ye be!
For I lo'ed nathing in all my lyfe,
　I daur weil say it, and honestly,

"But a fat horse and a fair woman,
　Twa bonny dogs to kill a deer;
But Ingland suld find me meal and maut
　Gif I had lived this hundred yeir.

"She suld haif fund me in meil and maut,
　And beif and mutton in all plentie;
But ne'er a Scots wyfe that could hae said
　That ever I skaithed her a puir flie.

"To seik het water under cauld ice,
　Surelie it is a great folie;
I haif asked grace at a gracelesse face,
　And there is nane for my men and me.

JOHNNIE ARMSTRONG

"But had I ken'd or I cam frae hame
    How thou unkind wadst be to me,
I wad hae kept the Border syde,
    In spite of a' thy peers and thee."

Gilnockie's spirited appeal availed him nothing. The end is best told in the words of the historian Pitscottie :

"The king hanged Johne Armstrang, Laird of Kilnokie, quhilk monie Scottis menne heavilie lamented, for he was ane doubtit (redoubtable) manne, and als gud ane Christane as ever was vpoun the Borderis. And albeit he was ane lous lewand man, and sustained the number of xxiiij weill-horsed able gentlemen with him, yitt he never molested no Scottis man. But it is said from the Scottis border to New Castle of Ingland, thaer was not ane of quhatsoever estate bot payed to this Johne Armestrang ane tribute, to be frie of his cumbir, he was so doubtit in Ingland."

Thirty-one others were hanged with gallant Johnnie on the trees of Carlanrig Chapel, about ten miles above Hawick on the road to Langholm.

If such a grisly performance as this was an episode in time of peace between the two countries, it may puzzle one to declare that such peace was preferable to open war. To enable you to form an opinion upon the nature of border warfare and its effect upon a people whose descendants at this day pursue their peaceful industry in the border lands, let me read two or three extracts from the official dispatches of the English warden, Lord Dacre, written in October, 1513, three months after the catastrophe of Flodden. These dispatches refer to no formal invasion of either country, when the utmost damage was done to property, but to the ordinary routine of frontier duty.

"On Tuesday at night last past I sent diverse of my tennents of Gillslande to the nombre of 60 personnes in Eskdalemuir upon the Middell Marches, and there brynt VII howses, tooke and brought away XXXVI hede of catell and much insight. On Weddinsday at thre of the clok efter noon, my broder, Sir Christopher assembled diverse of the king's subgjects beyng under my reull, and roode all that night into Scotland, and on Thursday in the mornynge, they began upon the said Middell Marches, and brynt the Stakeheugh (the manor-place of Irewyn) with the hamletts belonging to them down ; Irewyn bwrne, being the Chambrelain of Scotland owne lands, and undre his reull, continewally birnying from the breke of day to oone of the clok after noon, and there wan, tooke and brought away cccc hede of cattell, ccc shepe, certain horses and very much insight, and slew two men ; hurte and wounded diverse other persones and horses, and then entered Inglande ground again at vii of the clok that night."

Of course the Scots retaliated, and the English council rebuked Lord Dacre for want of vigilance.   Writing in May, 1514, he thus defends himself:

"For oone cattell taken by the Scotts, we have takyn, wan and brought away out of Scotland a hundreth; and for one sheep, two hundreth of a surity.   And as for townships and housis . . . I assure your lordships for truthe that I have, and hes caused, to be brynt and distroyed sex tymes moo townes and housis within . . .   Scotland in the same season then is done to us . . .   The watter of Liddell being xii myles of length, whereupon was a hundreth pleughis, . . . the water of Ewes being viii myles of length, whereupon was vii pleughes . . . lies all and every of them waist now, no corne sawn upon noone of the said groundis. . . .   Upon the West Marches I have burnt and distroyed the townships of Annand and 33 others, and the water of Esk from Stabulgorton down to Cannonby, being vi myles in length, whereas there was in all times past four hundreth ploughis and above, which er now clearly wasted and noo man dwelling in them in this day, save only in towris of Annand Steepel and Walghapp (Wauchope)."

Truly an awful picture of desolation, but no isolated one.   Listen to the report of Sir Thomas Warton, another English warden, thirty years later, of the mischief done by him in fifteen months of 1543 and 1544:

"Towns, Parish Churches, granges, and
hamlets burnt	-	-	-	-	316
Scotts slayne	-	-	-	-	438
Prisoners taken -	-	-	-	-	1,224

Oxen and kine driven off	-	-	-	13,671
Sheep	-	-	-	-	-	17,202
Goats	-	-	-	-	-	200
Horses	-	-	-	-	-	1,628

" Great quantity of insight brought away, over and besydes a greate quantite of corne and insight and a great nombre of all sortes of catail burned in the townes and howses, and menye menne also hurt."

You may observe that the English sovereign and his council did not insist, as it is the fashion to do now, upon correct spelling as an indispensable qualification for holding a commission !

Farming has not always been a very profitable industry on the Border, but imagine what it must have been in what some people sigh for as " the good old times." Read the ballad of *Jamie Telfer*, and it will help you to realise the sort of thing that might happen any night. I know that the higher criticism has been at work on this and other ballads. Truly spoke Walter Scott when he declared that if authors were the pillars of literature, critics were the caterpillars. They have endeavoured to undermine our faith in the genuine character of Border balladry ;

but, so far as I am concerned, my faith in them is unshaken. We know well enough that when Sir Walter Scott set himself to collect the fragments and variants of balladry floating to their death in the Border district, he aimed at forming a standard edition of them. He had to reconcile many discrepancies, to fill many *lacunæ*, to collate variant versions. But what he was better qualified to do than any other man was to preserve the action and spirit of the perishing minstrelsy. It is, I think, a vain waste of time and eyesight to point to an interpolated stanza here and a flaw in topography there. Who was the cynic who said that he preferred fiction to history, because in history nothing was true except names and dates, and in good fiction everything was true except the names and dates? I confess that I can find little patience for those who argue that such a rousing lay as *Jamie Telfer* cannot be genuine, because the names and dates do not square with exact genealogy and topography. Who cares whether Jamie could run so many miles within so many hours, or whether it was a Scott or an Elliot that befriended him?

Jamie Telfer o' the Fair Dodhead.

BORDER WARFARE

There are two main versions of this ballad, handed down from generation to generation among the people of both these clans, each making their own chiefs the heroes of the occasion ; just as in the ballads of *Otterbourne* and *Chevy Chase* you have two discrepant accounts of a single transaction, suited to the different prepossessions of Scots and English respectively. It is because the very spirit of border warfare pervades every line of this famous riding ditty and the process of " warning the water " so graphically set forth therein, that I venture to ask you to listen to a few stanzas from it. In my opinion the very ruggedness of the metre— the faultiness of the rhymes—are evidence of attrition through oral transmission, and stamp the composition as genuine.

> It fell aboot the Marti'mas tyde,
>   When our Border steeds get corn and hay,
> The Captain o' Bewcastle has bown' him ryde,
>   And he's ower to Tivi'dale to drive a prey.
>
> The first ae guide that they met wi',
>   It was high up Hardhaughswire ;
> The second guide that they met wi',
>   It was laigh doon in Borthwickwater.

JAMIE TELFER

"What tidings, what tidings, my trusty guide?"
  "Nae tidings, nae tidings I hae to thee;
But gin ye'll gae to the fair Dodhead,
  Mony a cow's calf I'll let thee see."

And when they cam to the fair Dodhead
  Right hastily they clamb the pele;
They loosed the kye oot, ane and a',
  And ranshackled the hoose right weel.

Now Jamie Telfer's heart was sair,
  The tear aye rowin' in his e'e;
He pled wi' the Captain to hae his gear,
  Or else revengit he wad be.

The Captain turn'd him round and leugh;
  Said—"Man, there's naething in thy house,
But ae auld sword without a sheath,
  That hardly now wad fell a mouse!"

The sun wasna up, but the mune was doon,
  It was the griming o' a new-fa'n snaw,
Jamie Telfer has run ten miles afoot,
  Between the Dodhead and the Stob's Ha'.

And when he cam to the fair tower yett,
  He shouted loud and weel cried he,
Till out bespak auld Gibbie Elliot—
  "Whae's this that brings the frae to me?"

"It's me, Jamie Telfer o' the fair Dodhead,
  And a harried man I think I be!
There's naething left in the fair Dodhead
  But a waefu' wife and bairnies three."

BORDER WARFARE

" Gae seek your succour at Branksome Ha',
    For succour ye'se get nane frae me !
 Gae seek your succour whaur ye paid black mail,
    For man ! ye ne'er paid money to me."

 Jamie Telfer has turned him roun' aboot,
    I wat the tear blinded his e'e—
" I'll ne'er pay mail to Elliot again,
    And the fair Dodhead I'll never see ! "

 He has turned him to the Tiviot side,
    E'en as fast as he could dri'e,
 Till he cam to the Coulthart cleugh,
    And there he shouted baith loud and hie.

 Then up bespak him auld Jock Grieve,
    " Whae's this that brings the fray to me ? "
" It's me, Jamie Telfer o' the fair Dodhead,
    A harried man I trow I be.

" There's naething left in the fair Dodhead
    But a greeting wife and bairnies three,
 And sax puir calves stand in the stall
    A' routing loud for their minnie."

" Alack and wae ! " quoth auld Jock Grieve,
    " Alack ! my heart is sair for thee !
 For I was married on the elder sister,
    And thou on the youngest o' a' the three."

 Then he's ta'en out a bonny black,
    Was right weel fed wi' corn and hay,
 And he's set Jamie Telfer on his back
    To the Catslockhill to tak the fray.

JAMIE TELFER

And when he cam to the Catslockhill,
　　He shouted loud and weel cried he,
Till out and spak him William's Wat—
　　"O whae's this brings the fray to me."

"It's me, Jamie Telfer o' the fair Dodhead,
　　A harried man I think I be!
The Captain o' Bewcastle has driven my gear,
　　For God's sake rise and succour me!"

"Alas for wae!" quo' William's Wat,
　　"Alack, for thee my heart is sair!
I never cam by the fair Dodhead
　　That ever I fand thy basket bare."

He's set his twa sons on coal-black steeds,
　　Himsel' upon a freckled gray,
And they are on wi' Jamie Telfer
　　To Branksome Ha' to tak the fray.

And whan they came to Branksome Ha',
　　They shouted a' baith loud and hie,
Till up and spak him bauld Buccleuch,
　　Said—"Whae's this brings the fray to me."

"It's me, Jamie Telfer o' the fair Dodhead,
　　And a harried man I think I be;
There's nocht left in the fair Dodhead
　　But a greeting wife and bairnies three."

"Alack for wae!" quo' the gude auld lord,
　　"And ever my heart is wae for thee.
But fy! gar cry on Willie my son,
　　And see that he come to me speedily.

BORDER WARFARE

"Gar warn the water, braid and wide,
 Gar warn it sune and hastily!
They that winna ride for Telfer's kye
 Let them never look in the face o' me!

"Warn Wat o' Harden and his sons,
 Wi' them will Borthwick water ride;
Warn Gaudilands and Allanhaugh
 And Gilmanscleuch and Commonside.

"Ride by the gate o' Priesthaughswire,
 And warn the Currors o' the Lee;
As ye come dune the Hermitage Slack
 Warn doughty Willie o' Gorrinberry."

The Scots they rade, the Scots they ran
 Sae starkly and sae steadily;
And aye the ower word o' the thrang
 Was—"Rise for Branksome readily!"[1]

The gear was driven the Frostylea up,
 Frae the Frostylea unto the plain,
Whan Willie has looked his men before
 And saw the kye right fast driving.

"Whae drives thir kye?" 'gan Willie say,
 "To mak an outspeckle o' me."
"It's me, the Captain o' Bewcastle, Willie;
 I winna layne my name fer thee."

---

[1] As aforesaid, there is a version of this ballad current
which transposes the parts assigned here to the Scotts
and the Elliots.

JAMIE TELFER

"O will ye let Telfer's kye gae back?
 Or will ye do aught for regard o' me?
Or, by faith o' my body!" quo' Willie Scott,
 "I'se ware my dame's calf-skin on thee!"

"I winna let the kye gae back,
 Neither for thy love, nor yet thy fear;
But I will drive Jamie Telfer's kye
 In spite of every Scot that's here!"

"Set on them, lads!" quo' Willie than;
 "Fy lads! set on them cruellie!
For e'er they win to the Ritterford,
 Mony a toom saddle there shall be!"

Then till't they gaed wi' heart and hand;
 The blows fell thick as bickering hail;
And mony a horse ran masterless,
 And mony a comely cheek was pale.

But Willie was stricken ower the head,
 And through the knapscap the sword has gane;
And Harden grat for very rage
 Whan Willie on the ground lay slain.

But he's ta'en aff his gude steel-cap,
 And thrice he waved it in the air:
The Dinlay snaw was ne'er mair white
 Than the lyart locks o' Harden's hair.

"Revenge, revenge!" auld Wat 'gan cry;
 "Fy lads! lay on them cruellie!
We'll ne'er see Tiviotside again
 Or Willie's death revenged shall be."

O mony a horse ran masterless,
   The splintered lances flew on hie ;
But or they wan to the Kershope ford,
   The Scots had gotten the victory.

I need not inflict upon you more of this ballad, with which, if you are not already familiar, let me assure you you ought to be. Suffice it to remind you that—

There was a wild gallant among us a'
   His name was Watty-wi'-the-Wudspurs,[1]
Cried—"On for his house in Stanegirthside,
   Gin ony man will ride wi' us !"

And on they went; not only did they recover Jamie Telfer's kye, but also they drove off the contents of the Captain o' Bewcastle's garth, so that—

Whan they cam back to the fair Dodhead
   They were a welcome sicht to see ;
For instead o' his ain ten milking kye
   Jamie Telfer has gotten thirty and three.

It was in a hard school such as this that our people were trained. We sometimes hear complaint of us Border folk that we are

---

[1] The Scottish synonym for "Hotspur."

dour, and that we are slow to see the point in jokes—in English jokes, at least. Well, no doubt we are lacking in that superficial polish which makes the social wheels run smooth; perhaps we are a trifle grim and do not take life as gaily as men of other lands; but a rough boyhood is apt to be followed by a thoughtful, stern manhood, and it takes some centuries to free a nation from the traces of early adversity. We may take credit for being richer and wiser and better educated than the people who had the making of Scotland, but is it quite certain that we should equal them in fortitude and resolution in similar arduous circumstances—in holding the marches of Tweed and Solway for three centuries against a far more powerful nation than ourselves?

Some such thoughts as these crowd into the mind of one standing amid these scenes of bygone strife. The land, so often blackened by the invader's fires, is now humming with peaceful industry; and around the bleached and roofless ruins of the great churches of our forefathers have risen many prosperous homesteads. The efforts once concentrated upon the work of cutting each others' throats are now applied to winning each others' votes. It grieves me that I should have allowed to escape from a treacherous memory the name of the bard who has moulded such reflections as these into a form far transcending the level of plodding prose.

> Long years of peace have stilled the battle thunder,
>   Wild grasses quiver where the fight was won ;
> Masses of blossom, lightly blown asunder,
>   Drop their white petals on the silent gun.
> For life is kind, and sweet things grow unbidden,
>   Turning the scenes of strife to verdant bowers ;
> Who shall declare what secrets may be hidden
>   Beneath that cloud of flowers ?
>
> Poor heart ! above thy field of sorrow sighing
>   For smitten faith and love untimely slain,
> Leave thou the soil wherein thy dead are lying
>   To the soft sunlight and the cleansing rain.
> Love works in silence, hiding all the traces
>   Of bitter conflict on the trampled sod,
> And time shall show thee all the battle places
>   Veiled by the hand of God.

Glasgow : Printed at the University Press by Robert MacLehose and Co. Ltd.